FABRIC PRINTING *at* HOME

Quick and Easy Fabric Design Using Fresh Produce and Found Objects

Julie B. Booth

Quarry Books
100 Cummings Center, Suite 406L
Beverly, MA 01915

quarrybooks.com • www.craftside.net

First published in the United States of America in 2015 by
Quarry Books, a member of
Quarto Publishing USA
100 Cummings Center
Suite 406-L
Beverly, Massachusetts 01915-6101
Telephone: (978) 282-9590
Fax: (978) 283-2742
www.quarrybooks.com
Visit www.craftside.net for a behind-the-scenes
peek at our crafty world!

10 9 8 7 6 5 4 3 2 1

ISBN: 978-1-59253-952-9

Digital edition published in 2015
eISBN: 978-1-62788-394-8

Library of Congress Cataloging-in-Publication Data available

Design: John Foster at badpeoplegoodthings.com
Photography: Pam Soorenko, except where otherwise noted
Cover Images: Pam Soorenko, except top center, middle, and bottom
center images, by Shutterstock.com

Printed in China

In memory of my dad, Mark T. Basseches,
who commissioned my first piece of art.

This book is dedicated to my mother, Janet, who always cheered me
on in all my artistic endeavors.

This book is also dedicated to my "boys."
To my husband Mark, my best friend and grounding force—thanks
for keeping me laughing and helping me to keep my sense of
perspective on this and other projects. You are the string to my kite!

To my son and "studio mate," Aaron, who had a front row seat to the
creation of all the artwork in this book—I continue to appreciate your
directness tempered by kindness. I'm so proud to be your mom.

contents

Introduction: Kitchen Potential 7

Chapter 1: Getting Started 11
Setting Up a Workspace.............................11
Assemble Your Basic Tool Kit 13
Paint Techniques....................................15

Chapter 2: Kitchen Textures
and Found Object Printing 29
Three Printing Techniques...........................30
Create a Collage Design with
Layered Textures.....................................30
Texture Squared......................................34
Found Objects and Kitchen Tools 44
Small Scale Items: Nine-Patch 46

Chapter 3: Beyond the Potato Print:
Using Vegetables and Fruit to Create
Fabric Designs 49
Creating Background Textures
with Vegetables......................................50
Making Marbled Fabric with
Cabbage Prints 53
Carving Print Blocks from Vegetables 54
Slicing and Dicing: Printing with
Vegetable Shapes....................................56
Lovely Leaves 58
Brayer Rubbings 59

Chapter 4: Wrap It Up! Wraps and Foil 61
Freezer Paper Fun: Masks and Stencils 62
Playing with Plastic Wrap 69
The Wonders of Wax Paper.........................70
Folk Art Foil: Embossed Designs
in Aluminum Foil......................................72

Chapter 5: Recycled and Repurposed 77
Cardboard: The Thick and Thin of It 78
Junk Mail Jackpot..84
On a Roll: Fabric Designs
from Cardboard Tubes 89
Making Your Mark: Designing Print Blocks
from Recycled Foam 90
Artful Aluminum: Create Decorative Shapes
from Recycled Cans and Pans 92
Printing with Recycled Materials...................94

Chapter 6: Irresistible: Fabric Resists
Using Kitchen Ingredients 97
Resist Recipes 98
Resist Application Techniques...................105
Painting a Resist-Covered Fabric 113
Setting Paint on Resist-Covered Fabric 113
Removing Resists 113

Chapter 7: Contributing Artists...............114

Resources 121

Acknowledgments 122

About the Author 123

Index..124

 INTRODUCTION

kitchen potential

The kitchen—in most people's homes it's a hub of activity. It's where we cook and eat our meals and find out about each other's day. Growing up, the kitchen was where I hung out with my friends. It's where I sometimes did homework and my messy art projects. It's where I watched my mom prepare dinners and learned how to bake. Most of you can probably conjure up some happy childhood memories that center around this important room.

I now spend my fair share of hours cooking and baking in my small but bright kitchen. I enjoy whipping up a batch of chocolate chip cookies and am known for my butterscotch brownies. But it wasn't until a few years ago that I realized that the kitchen could also be a resource for my artwork.

I'm always looking for new ways to create beautiful or intriguing fabric designs. I'm filled with curiosity and love to set challenges for myself. "What if?" is a predominant phrase in my artistic vocabulary. As a fiber arts and surface design teacher, I'm also constantly experimenting with available materials and trying to work out new printing techniques to share with my students. I enjoy reading books and articles and use them as jumping-off points for my own explorations (see the suggested book list in Resources on page 121).

When I began to teach a multiple-session class called "Exploring Surface Design," I knew that I had to expand my usual fabric printing repertoire. I was already using recycled materials, such as cardboard and Styrofoam, for print blocks in my classes. I encouraged students to find materials at home to bring into class for texture blocks. What I needed was a class session about resist techniques. What I wanted were no-frills fabric resists—ones that were easily accessible to students. For example, I first discovered freezer paper when I started making cloth dolls. I was taught to draw doll patterns on this paper and iron the plastic-coated paper pieces directly onto my fabric. I saw the potential for using this material to mask off areas of the fabric from paint. This two-sided paper became the first kitchen product to be added to my resist list. Thanks to a magazine article by fiber artist Jane Dunnewold, I found out about wheat flour paste resist. A simple recipe of white wheat flour and water and this resist mimics the crackle patterns of traditional batik. It soon became a staple in my surface design class. Blue school glue, glue stick, and salt rounded out the resist list.

It didn't stop there. I started to further experiment with these few basic resist materials. I began printing, stenciling, and making rubbings with them. I started using more than one resist on a piece of fabric. My curiosity was piqued and I began to wonder what other kitchen materials could be used as resists?

To answer this question, I applied for and won a grant from my local fiber guild. For eighteen months I experimented with household materials to see which ones could work as fabric resists.

Chapter 6, "Irresistible: Fabric Resists Using Kitchen Ingredients," has some of the successful recipes and application techniques based on my research.

Since my grant, I continue to return to the kitchen as a surface design resource. I get a little giddy every week as I rifle through the recyclables looking for sturdy postcards, cardboard boxes, and envelopes with little cellophane windows. I'm constantly eyeing plastic bottles and bottle caps, wondering about their printing potential. I keep contemplating new ways to print with food wraps. And, of course, no vegetable is safe in my house!

How to Use This Book

My intention in writing this book is to get you excited! Most of the items you need to create beautiful fabrics are just a few steps away, in your kitchen. I want you to begin looking at the products and materials in your kitchen with new eyes. Check out your recycling bin for paper products, plastic bottles, aluminum cans, and pans. Look in the kitchen drawers for interesting found objects, plastic wrap, wax paper, and aluminum foil. Don't forget the fruit and vegetable bin or your kitchen staples—all have surface design potential.

In addition to your kitchen finds, you'll need some basic fabric painting and printing supplies. Chapter 1 reviews what you need to set up a portable work area as well as a basic tool kit. You'll learn about fabric, paint, and printing tools.

Chapters 2 through 6 each focus on a particular category of kitchen supply or product. These chapters are chock-full of suggested techniques for using kitchen items to create print blocks and plates, stencils, masks, and fabric resists along with many helpful hints and tips to get the best printing results. Chapters 2 through 6 are stand-alone chapters. Feel free to start with any one of them.

Now—go make some awesome fabrics!

getting started

After many years of using my dining room table for printing fabric, it was time to invest in a more permanent studio space. Before deciding on the specifics of my own workspace, I went to see other textile artists' studios to get ideas. Each studio was different but all had things in common.

With my son off at college, the family room seemed like the perfect place to set up shop. I turned four adjustable folding tables into one large worktable with the help of a 5' x 8' (152 x 244 cm) piece of plywood (my flat surface). I attached two layers of padding to the plywood—carpet padding and a large fleece blanket. The padded table was then covered with a thick plastic drop cloth to protect the surface from occasional paint spills. I invested in good lighting and shelving for storage. Finally, a place I could call my own!

Setting Up a Workspace

It doesn't take much to set up a perfectly workable area for painting and printing fabric. A dining room or kitchen table, a wide counter, or a folding table are all good solutions. Or put together some easy-to-store padded portable work surfaces (see "Assembling a Padded Portable Work Surface" on page 14). If you can't afford or don't have good overhead (artificial) lighting, a room with strong natural light and a lamp with an all-spectrum bulb are good alternatives. If you don't have the space for large shelving units, get creative with baskets and boxes to store supplies. Don't think you need the perfect studio space to create beautiful painted and printed fabrics!

My studio, pictured here, has all the essentials for a good workspace, allowing me to make prints, such as the one opposite, which uses found objects such as batteries and milk bottle caps.

A. dense foam brayer **B.** glass palette **C.** foam dauber **D.** palette knife **E.** small plastic container **F.** fabrics (Prepared for Dyeing and light-colored cotton) **G.** plastic spoons **H.** wipe-up cloth **I.** paper towels **J.** plastic container for water **K.** pins **L.** foam brushes **M.** bristle brushes **N.** fabric paints **O.** mister **P.** masking tape **Q.** padded portable work surface

Assemble Your Basic Tool Kit

Below is a list of the tools and materials needed for most of the projects in this book. I like to call it your Basic Tool Kit. You'll need these supplies handy before you get started.

- Padded portable work surface(s).
- Prepared for Dyeing (PFD) cotton or pre-washed white or light-colored 100 percent cotton fabric cut into fat quarters.
- Masking tape or pins to attach the fabric to the padded work surface.
- Fabric paints (such as Pebeo Setacolor). You will use both transparent and opaque paints. Specific techniques will require one or the other. I suggest you have at least white (available only in opaque), black, and the primary colors.
- Small plastic containers with lids to hold paint. I often use disposable, plastic 8-ounce (235 ml) containers, but recycled yogurt, margarine, or other small containers work well, too.
- Plastic spoons or palette knives for mixing paint and spooning it out.
- Foam brushes in 1" (2.5 cm) and 2" (5 cm) sizes.
- Foam dauber.
- Bristle brushes in assorted sizes.
- Water container for water to dilute transparent paints. I use a 1½ quart (1.4 L) plastic pitcher.
- Additional recycled plastic containers to hold spoons, brushes, and so on.
- Plant mister or spray bottle with water.
- At least two or three dense foam brayers.

- At least two or three glass or Plexiglas palettes, edges taped with duct tape.
- Paper towels.
- Extra fabric (such as cotton or muslin) to be used as wipe-up cloths and for sampler fabrics (optional, but recommended).

Now let's take a more in-depth look at some of the items in your Basic Tool Kit.

PADDED PORTABLE WORK SURFACE

Padded portable work surfaces are easy to create (see "Assembling a Padded Portable Work Surface" on page 14) and store. They are light enough to easily transport. Make them large enough to fit a fat quarter of fabric. Even though I have a large worktable, I use these padded boards all the time. I'm often painting or printing a number of fabric pieces so I like to keep several of these work surfaces handy.

FABRIC CHOICES AND SIZES

For the techniques covered in this book, we will use 100 percent cotton fabric. I recommend PFD cotton, which can be used right off the bolt. It has no sizing, nor has it been treated with optical whiteners. As an alternative, try white or light-to-medium solid colors of 100 percent cotton fabric. Pre-wash in warm or hot water with a detergent that has no softeners or other additives. We will be using fabric paints rather than dyes for the techniques in this book, so this basic fabric pre-treatment will be enough to allow the paints to coat the surface of the fabric.

OTHER CONSIDERATIONS

The following are important for a workspace to paint and print fabric:

- A flat surface (kitchen or dining room table, wide counter, folding table)
- Padding (a blanket, large towel, thin quilt batting, doubled felt) placed on a flat surface
- Plastic covering to protect the surface (a drop cloth, plastic tablecloth, vinyl, plastic film/acetate)
- Good lighting (full spectrum, natural light)
- Storage for supplies (shelving, plastic storage boxes, baskets)

ASSEMBLING A PADDED PORTABLE WORK SURFACE

Following are materials to create one board:

- One 20" x 30" (51 x 76 cm) foam core board or piece of heavy corrugated cardboard.
- Two pieces of 20" x 30" (51 x 76 cm) white acrylic craft felt (you can substitute with thin quilt batting).
- One 20" x 30" (51 x 76 cm) piece of plastic film or acetate (.003 thickness). Buy this in either 12' (3.7 m) or 50' (15 m) rolls. You can also use heavy vinyl, a plastic drop cloth, or even trash bags cut to fit the board. I prefer the plastic film because it is a smooth surface without wrinkles or folds.
- 2" (5 cm) -wide masking tape.
- Scissors for cutting the felt and plastic.

INSTRUCTIONS

1. Cut the felt and plastic to fit the foam core board.

2. Lay the pieces of felt on the foam core board and attach securely with the 2" (5 cm) -wide masking tape.

3. Attach a piece of plastic film to the padded board using a few pieces of strategically placed tape.

Cut two pieces of acrylic felt to the same size as the foam core board.

Roll out and cut enough plastic film or acetate to cover the padded foam core board.

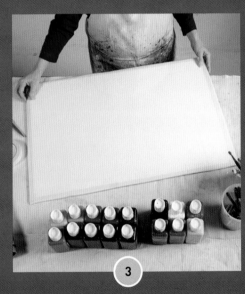

Tape the plastic film to the board with a few pieces of masking tape.

You will be able to print up to a fat quarter (18" x 22.5" [46 x 57 cm]) at a time using your padded portable work surfaces. When I'm experimenting with a technique for the first time, I often work smaller. Try cutting some 15" x 20" (38 x 51 cm) or 12" x 15" (31 x 38 cm) swatch sizes for your experiments or to make sampler fabrics.

FABRIC PAINTS

Fabric paints are acrylic-based with a special binder to help them adhere to the fabric. The best quality fabric paints can be painted and printed without affecting the feel or "hand" of the fabric. Most brands have both transparent and opaque versions of paint. Transparent fabric paints are usually diluted before use. Similar to watercolor paints, transparent fabric paints can be blended on the fabric by overlaying washes of color. Opaque fabric paints are thicker and used for printing and stenciling.

Paint Techniques

Try the following paint techniques using transparent and opaque paints.

USING TRANSPARENT FABRIC PAINTS

Read the paint container label for information on the recommended ratio of water to paint to get the proper dilution to most easily apply it to fabric. I like to use Pebeo Setacolor; the basic dilution is one part paint to two parts water. Transparent fabric paint can be used in different dilutions for different techniques or effects. It can be used undiluted or slightly diluted when printing with embossed aluminum foil printing plates, wax paper printing plates, or when monoprinting with plastic wrap (see chapter 4). For painting over dried fabric resists, use a slightly thicker than recommended dilution to prevent the paint from breaching the resist (see chapter 6). To achieve a pastel color wash, more water

is required. In that case, it's best to mix undiluted paints in a separate container. Thin the paint by adding an equal amount of water. Fill a different container with water and gradually stir in the thinned paint until you get the pastel color desired.

MIXING CUSTOM COLORS WITH TRANSPARENT FABRIC PAINTS

To mix a custom color, start with undiluted paint. To avoid wasting paint, first pour a lighter color into a plastic container and gradually mix in a darker color. Some colors, such as red and black, are so saturated that mere drops can quickly and dramatically change the paint color. After mixing the undiluted colors, add water. Water will lighten the color so you should take that into account when mixing the undiluted paints.

TIP: One Paint Job—Two Fabrics

Here's a quick way to create two pieces of painted fabric. After painting a piece of fabric (see pages 16–17) carefully lay a second piece of unpainted fabric on top. Roll a dense foam brayer across the back of the second piece to pick up the paint from the first piece. Peel off the second fabric and lay it on a portable work surface to dry. The second piece picks up color from the first plus texture from the brayer, making for a great background fabric!

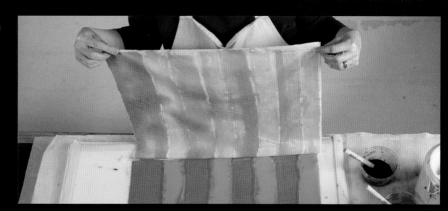

To quickly create a second background fabric, lay a dry white piece of fabric over a just-painted fabric, roll a dense foam brayer across it, and peel off.

Painting Fabric Backgrounds with Transparent Fabric Paints

Although it's possible to use commercial solid color fabric for the techniques in chapters 2 through 6, why not add a personal touch by painting your own color backgrounds? Hand-painted backgrounds can add texture, depth, and variety to your fabric designs. Depending on the effect you wish to achieve for your background, you can use analogous colors such as blue and violet or contrasting colors such as blue and yellow. You can also decide whether you want to use the recommended dilution or create a pastel color. Here are a few ideas for hand-painted backgrounds.

INSTRUCTIONS

1. Cut the fabric into fat quarter pieces or use a smaller size to experiment. Tape a piece of fabric to a padded portable work surface.

2. If using a solid color, lightly mist the fabric before painting, which can help the paint flow more freely from the brush onto the fabric. Misting is also a way to blend colors. If you are painting a design and want more defined edges between colors, do not mist the fabric.

3. Dip a foam brush into the diluted paint. If using a clean brush, let it sit in the container briefly to better soak up paint and then brush it across the edge of the container to release excess paint. (See A.)

Dip a foam brush into one of the containers of paint. Brush it across the container's edge to release excess paint before painting the fabric.

Paint stripes with the first paint color, leaving space on the fabric for the second color.

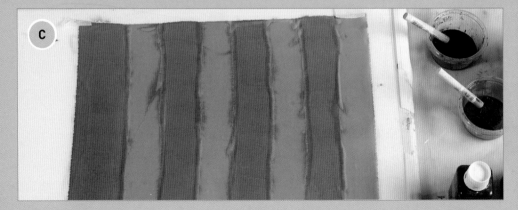

This finished background fabric features stripes in blue and violet.

MATERIALS

- two colors of diluted transparent fabric paint
- foam paint brushes
- masking tape
- Prepared for Dyeing (PFD) cotton or pre-washed white 100 percent cotton fabric
- padded portable work surface(s)
- wipe-up cloth
- plant mister or spray bottle (optional)
- clean dense foam brayer (optional)

4. To paint the fabric one solid color, paint a brush-width of color at a time, dipping your brush into the paint as needed until the fabric is completely and evenly covered with paint.

5. For stripes, paint all the stripes of one color first and then go back in to paint the second color. For more defined lines, do not mist the fabric. Leave some unpainted space between the first and second colors; the second color will bleed slightly to meet the first color. To mix the paints, paint the second color along the edge of the first color or mist with the spray bottle. For variety, paint blocks or shapes of color or leave some of the white fabric unpainted. Use an extra piece of cloth to wipe up excess paint on your work surface. (See B and C.)

6. To get rid of air pockets that might show up on the fabric while painting, roll a clean dense foam brayer (see "Foam Brayer" under "Paint Application Techniques" on page 18) across the fabric. Wipe up excess paint with a wipe-up cloth.

USING OPAQUE FABRIC PAINTS

Opaque fabric paints are thicker than transparent paints and are not diluted before use. In the chapters that follow, you will learn how to use these paints with print blocks and stencils to create rich fabrics full of texture, pattern, and imagery.

MIXING CUSTOM COLORS WITH OPAQUE FABRIC PAINTS

Just as with the transparent paint colors, it is much more economical to start with the lightest opaque color in the mixture and gradually add darker colors. To brighten up colors, start with a bit of opaque white and add other colors to it. Adding just a little white gives a printed color a bit of spark compared with using a color right out of the container, which often appears flat when printed.

To make a color tint, mix up a base color in a container. Pour some white paint into a separate container and gradually add the base color until it is the desired tint color. Test the tint color on your fabric before printing. Colors appear lighter in the container than on the fabric. To test a color, dip your pinkie in the paint and put a small dot in an inconspicuous spot on the fabric. Use a similar technique for mixing shades or cool or warm tones of a base color.

Roll a paint-covered dense foam brayer across a print block until it is evenly coated with paint and press the block onto the fabric. This technique creates the most uniform fabric prints.

PAINT APPLICATION TECHNIQUES

Below are three ways to apply opaque fabric paint to print blocks. Each application technique has certain advantages and will give particular surface effects.

Foam Brayer

A dense foam brayer (or roller) has a solid wood core under heavy foam that makes it ideal for picking up paint and transferring it to a print block. You will also need a glass or Plexiglas palette for this technique. A palette is a smooth flat surface on which to roll out paint. Framing shops or craft stores with framing departments often have pre-cut glass that can easily be turned into a printing palette by taping the sharp edges with duct tape.

1. Spoon ¼ teaspoon paint onto a glass palette and roll the foam brayer back and forth to spread the paint until there is an even coat of paint on the brayer.

2. Roll the paint-covered brayer back and forth over the print block until it is evenly coated.

3. Press the block onto the fabric to release the paint from the block.

4. Reapply paint to the block after each print, about ¼ teaspoon at a time. Don't overload the palette. Too much paint on the palette will mean too much paint on the brayer and the result is a messy print.

This application technique makes the most uniform-looking fabric prints. It works best on print blocks that have a relatively flat surface or elements that are of uniform height.

Foam Brush

This application technique works well with both flat and more dimensional texture blocks. Prints using this technique can have a slightly streaked look from the brush strokes. An advantage to using this technique is that you can easily apply more than one color to the print block at the same time. You can also print a block using one brushed-on color and then paint details on the same block in one or more colors before overprinting.

1. Mix up opaque fabric paint in a small plastic container.

2. Dip a 1" or 2" (2.5 or 5 cm) foam brush into the paint and brush it across the edge of the container to release excess paint. Try not to have too much paint on the brush or you will get too much on the print block, resulting in messy prints.

3. Lightly brush the paint across the block. To prevent messy prints, try to paint only the topmost surface of the design and avoid getting paint into the crevices of the block.

4. Turn the block over onto the fabric and press to release the paint.

Using a foam brush allows you to apply more than one color to the block. Prints will have some texture from the brush strokes.

Foam Dauber

Sponge paint onto a print block using a foam dauber made from soft upholstery foam (see "How to Make a Foam Dauber" on page 21). Use this application technique for more dimensional blocks, such as the kitchen staples and baker's clay blocks in chapter 2. Unlike the other application techniques, it's okay for paint to get into the lower surfaces of the block design. Apply multiple colors for added interest.

1. Spoon ¼ teaspoon opaque paint onto a glass palette.

2. Press the dauber into the paint and then press it against the glass a few times to release excess paint.

3. Daub paint onto the block until it is completely and evenly covered.

4. Press the print block onto the fabric to release the paint.

Use a foam dauber to apply paint to more dimensional blocks. This technique allows you to apply more than one color to the block before printing.

HOW TO MAKE A FOAM DAUBER

A foam dauber is an easy-to-make printing tool requiring only upholstery foam and a rubber band. It's the perfect tool for applying fabric paint to dimensional print blocks, including carved vegetables (chapter 3), and to stencils (chapters 4 and 5). Make a number of these to have handy for printing with different paint colors.

MATERIALS

- ½" (1.3 cm) -thick upholstery foam (the soft spongy foam)
- rubber bands (one for each dauber you make)
- scissors
- thick permanent marker
- clear plastic gridded ruler

INSTRUCTIONS

1. Use the ruler and permanent marker to mark 4" x 6" (10 x 15 cm) rectangles on the foam.

2. Use scissors to cut out the rectangle from the foam.

3. Fold one of the long sides of the foam rectangle to the middle. Fold the other long side of the foam rectangle over the first.

4. Fold the foam in half. Secure it with a rubber band.

1

For each dauber, measure and mark a 4" x 6" (10 x 15 cm) rectangle on ½" (1.3 cm) soft upholstery foam.

2

Cut out the foam rectangle.

3

Fold the long edges, one at a time, to the center.

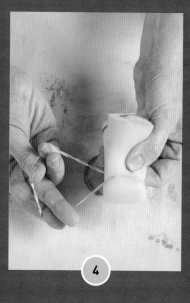

4

Fold in half and secure it with a rubber band.

SETTING PAINT

For the fabric paint to adhere permanently to the fabric, it needs to be set. Read the directions on the paint container label for specific information on how to set the paint. Most fabric paint is set by heat using either an iron or clothes dryer. When using an iron to heat-set fabric, have an extra piece of cotton or muslin to use as a pressing cloth. Lay this piece of cloth on top of the painted fabric to protect the iron.

In my experience, some fabric paints set passively over time. To test whether a particular brand of fabric paint can do this, paint a number of fabric swatches the same color. Set one swatch aside as the control that will not be washed out. Every couple of days, place a different swatch in warm soapy water to see whether the paint washes out. If no paint appears in the soapy water, then you know that the paint has set without heat. The brand of paint I use (Pebeo Setacolor) takes a week to passively set. Choose a dark paint color to better see whether paint is washing out of the fabric.

KEEPING TOOLS CLEAN

Fabric paint is acrylic-based and can be easily cleaned up with soap and water. Just as with other acrylic paints, it's important to clean tools before the fabric paint dries. If paint dries on a foam brush, it will become stiff and impossible to use. If you are unable to wash paint brushes immediately, keep them sitting in wet paint or put them in a container with water to prevent them from drying.

Rinse foam brayers with warm water and a bit of liquid dishwashing soap. Rub to remove paint. The paint will stain the foam and over time there may be some paint buildup, but this will not hinder the effectiveness of the brayer.

Carved erasers and commercial print blocks made from rubber-like material (such as Speedy Carve) are easy to clean. Rinse under running water and use a mild liquid dishwashing soap if needed. If paint is stuck in crevices, try using a soft toothbrush to carefully remove it. The paints do have a tendency to stain these types of blocks. Blocks made from materials that are coated with a sealant and those made from other materials such as recycled foam or aluminum are best cleaned before the fabric paint dries on them. Lightly mist the block and carefully wipe off the paint with a paper towel. For blocks that have more fragile components, create a moist stamping pad by folding over a couple of paper towels and misting them with water. Print the paint-covered blocks on this damp pad of paper towels until most of the paint comes off.

Once you have a designated space to work, some padded portable work surfaces, and the basic tools and materials for painting and printing fabric, it's time to move forward to discover the exciting fabric printing secrets hidden in the drawers, cupboards, refrigerator, and recycling bin of your kitchen.

TIP: Drying Fabrics

Set up a designated area for drying wet painted or printed fabrics. Because the fabrics are attached to portable work surfaces, they can be easily moved to a separate area for drying. By keeping the painting/printing and the drying areas separate, you can continue working on additional fabrics. Place wet fabrics near a heater or run a fan to help them dry more quickly.

To create an effective background treatment for kitchen-inspired fabrics, begin with alternating stripes of transparent paint followed by overprinting with a texture block of opaque paint. This fabric combines printing with an embossed baker's clay texture block and a colorful arrangement of carved fruits and vegetables.

A. self-healing cutting mat **B.** fabric scissors **C.** craft knife **D.** small, sharp scissors **E.** tin snips **F.** linoleum cutting tool

G. linoleum cutting tool tips **H.** rotary cutters

Other Helpful Equipment, Tools, and Supplies

In addition to the Basic Tool Kit, each project or technique described in the following chapters will list other items you will need, including the following:

EQUIPMENT

- Iron and ironing board or pad
- Washing machine and dryer
- Stove or hot plate
- Microwave
- Large sink
- Computer printer that can enlarge and reduce copies or a photocopier

CUTTING TOOLS

- Craft or other small utility knife
- Rotary cutter
- Fabric scissors, utility scissors, and small sharp scissors for paper cut designs
- Linoleum cutting tool and tips
- Tin snips
- Self-healing cutting mat (to use with craft knife and rotary cutter)

MEASURING AND MARKING TOOLS

- Clear plastic gridded ruler
- Measuring tape
- Washable marker
- Disappearing marker
- Thick and thin permanent markers
- Graphite pencil
- Measuring cups for liquid and dry measurements
- Measuring spoons

ADHESIVES

- Masking tape (both 1" and 2" [2.5 and 5 cm]), blue painter's tape, double-sided tape
- White glue (such as Mod Podge)
- Gel medium
- Tacky glue
- Glue stick
- Hot glue gun and hot glue sticks

PAPER

- White printer paper
- Black construction paper
- Tracing paper

A. wire whisk **B.** large metal spoon **C.** corncob holders **D.** plastic spreader **E.** decorative hole punches
F. stencils **G.** trivet **H.** cookie cutters

MISCELLANEOUS

Below is a list of tools that will come in handy for designing print blocks and stencils, as well as working with a variety of fabric resists.

- Pillow case or drawstring laundry bag
- Rubber bands
- Corncob holders
- Cookie cutters for cutting vegetable slices and for templates
- Commercial stencils
- Decorative hole punches
- "Tools" for incising foam, embossing foils, and scratching designs in resists: wooden skewer, fork, and ballpoint pen
- Plastic spreader or small squeegee
- Plastic squeeze bottles for applying resists
- Large bowl (such as a 1¾-quart [1.7 L] Pyrex bowl)
- Wire whisk
- 3-quart (2.8 L) cooking pot
- Large metal spoon
- Trivet
- Plastic tub that fits in a large sink

Use miscellaneous marking tools such as a fork or ballpoint pen to create incised designs in recycled foam blocks. Print different blocks together for a rich, textural fabric such as the one shown here (see "Making Your Mark: Designing Print Blocks from Recycled Foam" on page 90).

kitchen textures and found object printing

Found object printing feels a lot like being on a scavenger hunt. When I'm looking for potential patterns, I dig through the kitchen catchall drawer, peer into cupboards, check under the sink, and inspect the recyclables. For the projects in this chapter, I also made a trip to the grocery and local dollar stores in search of more texture treasures to use for fabric designs.

Texture typically plays a supporting role in my fabric designs. It is the first layer I print, and it usually blends in with the color of the fabric, making a more interesting background on which to print additional layers of patterns or images. But for this chapter, texture is the star. Fabrics in this chapter feature multiple layers of texture printing using blocks created from food staples, string, and stencils made from shelf liners and doilies. You will learn how to make brayer rubbings and create embossed texture blocks using baker's clay. We will print with found objects and kitchen tools and carve designs in erasers of all sizes and shapes. You will learn how to design fabrics that focus on repetition, layers, and patterning. I hope you will feel the excitement of exploring the vast potential of using these everyday materials to create your own beautiful fabrics.

The printed fabric collage opposite is full of movement and color created by printing, stenciling, and rubbing with a variety of kitchen textures.

TEXTURED MATERIALS SUGGESTIONS

Keep a lookout for these flat, textured materials that are great for direct printing, brayer rubbing, and some stenciling:

- Nonslip crisper liners
- Vinyl lace tablecloths
- Placemats (embossed plastic or vinyl and natural materials such as bamboo)
- Gripper pads
- Silicone pot holders
- Cake fondant texture sheets
- Netted fruit and vegetable bags

Once you have a varied assortment of texture finds, it's time to divide them into categories to best unravel their secrets: materials that are generally flat with an overall embossed, raised, or open design (such as doilies), non slip shelf liners, or netting; materials that have a random textured surface and are easy to handle (such as sponges and pot scrubbers); and materials that work best when adhered to a backing material, including kitchen staples and string. This first section focuses on the first two categories of texture: flat, embossed materials and those with a textured surface.

Three Printing Techniques

We will use the following fabric printing techniques throughout the course of this book.

Direct printing: Fabric paint is applied directly to the object, print block, or textured material using a paint-covered foam brayer, foam brush, or foam dauber (see page 20). The paint-covered material is then turned over onto the fabric and pressed (or in the case of cardboard tube designs, rolled across the fabric) to release the paint onto the fabric.

Stenciling: Create a stencil by cutting designs in sturdy, flat materials, such as shelf liners, cereal boxes (see "Cardboard Stencils" on page 82), or freezer paper (see "Freezer Paper Stencils" on page 64). You can also use materials that have open areas or designs such as sink mats or doilies. Place the stencil onto the fabric and apply paint through the open areas of the design using a paint-covered foam dauber, foam brush, or foam brayer. Lift the stencil to reveal the design.

Brayer rubbing: With this method, flat, textured materials or textures adhered to a flat piece of cardboard (see "Brayer Rubbings with the Blocks" on page 43) are slipped under the fabric. A paint-covered foam brayer is rolled across the fabric covering the materials to pick up the textures.

Create a Collage Design with Layered Textures

Working with flat, textured materials is particularly inspiring. By combining direct printing, stenciling, and brayer rubbing in different sequences, you can come up with surprising results. A printed texture collage is the perfect way to showcase these discoveries.

MATERIALS

- nonslip shelf liner or crisper liner
- craft knife or small, sharp scissors
- permanent marker
- clear plastic gridded ruler
- self-healing cutting mat

CUTTING STENCIL DESIGNS AND SHAPES FROM A NONSLIP SHELF LINER

Before printing your collage, you will need to create stencils and shapes to print.

INSTRUCTIONS

1. Measure rectangular shapes with the ruler and cut them out of the shelf liner. Rectangles or squares 4" to 6" (10 to 15 cm) are a good size. You can also opt to cut organic shapes.

2. Mark simple designs such as circles, ovals, or squares on the shapes with the permanent marker. Center the design, making sure there is at least a 1" (2.5 cm) border surrounding it.

3. On a cutting mat, use the craft knife or scissors to carefully cut out the design. Try to cut it out all in one piece and save the cut shapes for brayer rubbings or direct printing.

Cut rectangles or other shapes out of a shelf liner.

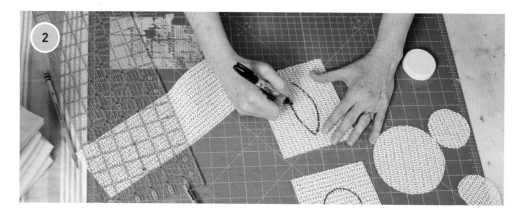

Draw simple designs on the shelf liner shapes.

Cut out the designs.

Combine layers of direct printing, stenciling, and brayer rubbings to create a colorful fabric, such as the one here.

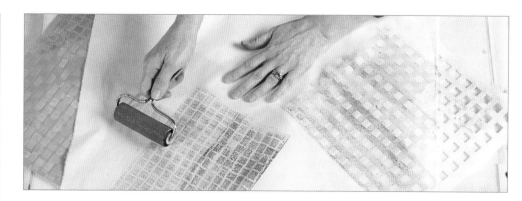

PRINTING YOUR COLLAGE DESIGN

Combine your shelf liner stencils with other flat and textured kitchen materials to print a colorful "collage" on fabric.

Before starting, mix up a selection of opaque fabric paint colors or use colors directly from the bottles. Choose two to three base colors and then mix tints of those colors. (See "Mixing Custom Colors with Opaque Fabric Paints" on page 17.) Start your fabric collage with brayer rubbings (for ideas, see "Facing the Blank Canvas," below).

Try brayer rubbings with flat kitchen textures to add an interesting background to your fabric. Slip flat-textured materials under the fabric and roll a paint-covered dense foam brayer across the fabric to pick up the designs.

1. Tape your fabric to your work surface and slip a selection of flat-textured materials under it.

2. Spoon about ¼ teaspoon opaque fabric paint onto the glass palette. Roll the foam brayer back and forth until it is evenly coated with paint.

3. Roll the paint-covered brayer across part of the fabric, using just enough pressure to pick up the texture underneath. Change paint colors and roll over other textures. (See above image.)

4. Continue adding layers to your texture collage with direct printing and basic stenciling (see "Three Printing Techniques" on page 30). Experiment with combining direct printing with a shelf liner stencil and sponging a contrasting color through the opening. Or layer flat textures and stencils under the fabric for more elaborate brayer rubbings.

FACING THE BLANK CANVAS

It's the old cliché, but so often the case that looking at a white piece of fabric can be as intimidating as a blank canvas. That is one reason why I often start my fabric designs with washes of transparent fabric paint (see "Painting Fabric Backgrounds with Transparent Fabric Paints" on page 16). Adding large swaths of texture with brayer rubbings is another answer to the blank canvas dilemma (see "Three Printing Techniques" on page 30).

Texture Squared

Take a look in your pantry and no doubt you will find bags and boxes of fabric-designing treasures. Turn dried kidney beans, lentils, rice, nuts, and pasta into unique texture print blocks. You can then "square" those texture block designs by using them to create embossed baker's clay blocks. Print them together for a graphic play of positive and negative shapes. Slip blocks under your fabric and roll over them with paint for texture rubbings. Fabrics made with these techniques can stand on their own or become the perfect background for additional layers of printing or stenciling.

TEXTURE BLOCKS FROM KITCHEN STAPLES

Some kitchen materials are too small to print individually. Instead it is easier to print these items by attaching them to a cardboard backing. Print these blocks for an overall background texture or repeating design.

INSTRUCTIONS

1. Pour glue or gel medium into the plastic container and brush a thin layer onto the cardboard.

2. Arrange the textured materials on the cardboard. Pour and push small items, such as rice and lentils, into the glue for an even layer. Place larger materials, such as kidney beans or almonds, individually on the glue. Break spaghetti into smaller pieces and arrange them to form designs. Attach string, toothpicks, and paper clips to cardboard blocks using double-sided tape.

3. Wait a few minutes and then tip the block to remove excess material. Check to see that there are no obvious empty spots on the block. If there are, sprinkle on more material to fill them in.

4. Seal the texture blocks by brushing on at least one layer of glue. This will also help to further secure the items to the cardboard. Let the glue dry completely on the blocks before printing or using them to emboss baker's clay (see "Embossed Texture Blocks Using Baker's Clay" on page 38).

MATERIALS

- corrugated cardboard cut into pieces at least 3" x 4" (7.5 x 10 cm)
- craft knife
- clear plastic gridded ruler
- self-healing cutting mat
- textured kitchen staples (such as rice, lentils, kidney beans, pasta, and tree nuts)
- other kitchen items (such as toothpicks, string or twine, and paper clips)
- white glue (such as Mod Podge) or gel medium
- plastic container
- foam brush
- plastic or other table covering
- double-sided tape
- masking tape

1

Brush the glue onto the cardboard.

2

Pour or place materials onto the wet glue.

3

Allow the glue to set for a few minutes before tipping the block to remove excess materials.

4

After the block is completely dry, add another layer of white glue to seal the block.

WRAP AROUND KITCHEN TEXTURES

Here are three ideas for making texture blocks by wrapping materials around corrugated cardboard:

1. Rubber Band Block. A simple print block with graphic punch! Wrap rubber bands around a piece of cardboard. Try different size rubber bands. Print either side of the block.

2. Twist-Tie Block. Create a texture print with thin loopy lines using twist-tie material. Use double-sided tape on the front of the cardboard block to help secure the twist-tie. If there are any loose twist-tie ends, secure them to the back of the block with masking tape.

Print bold lines with this easy-to-make rubber-band texture block.

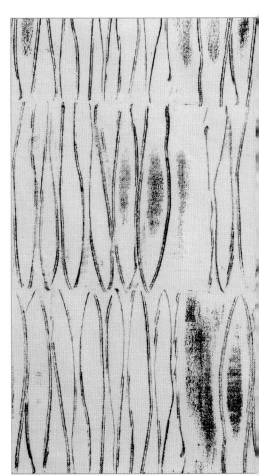

Print an organic background design using the irregular loops of twist-tie prints.

3. String or Twine Blocks. Manipulate string or twine on cardboard to print a range of textures and designs. Tape a layer of double-sided tape to the front side of the cardboard to help secure the string or twine. Wrap, knot, or braid lengths of string or twine. Tape loose ends to the back of the cardboard.

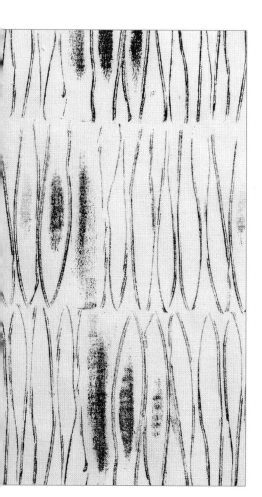
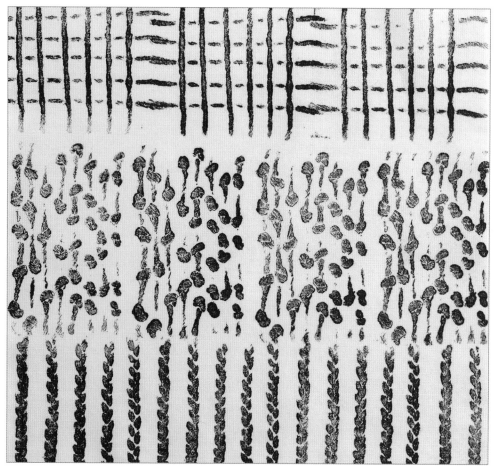

Wrap, knot, or braid—textures made with string and twine can take on many appearances.

Embossed Texture Blocks Using Baker's Clay

Use the kitchen staples blocks you just created to make embossed baker's clay blocks. A simple recipe made from all-purpose flour, salt, and water, baker's clay is most often used to make holiday ornaments. It also works wonderfully for embossing textures. After the clay blocks are baked and sealed, they will be ready to print. The printed images will appear as the negative of the kitchen staples textures, making for an interesting textural and graphic contrast with the original blocks.

Baker's Clay Recipe
This recipe makes approximately ten 3" x 4" (7.5 x 10 cm) print blocks.

INSTRUCTIONS

1. Mix the flour, salt, and water in a large bowl until almost uniform. Then knead the dough for a few minutes until it is smooth. Split the dough into three equal parts. You will work with one piece of dough at a time.

2. Place the first piece of dough between two sheets of wax paper. (Optional: Sprinkle flour on the bottom sheet of wax paper to prevent the dough from sticking to it.) Roll out the dough to ⅛" (3 mm) thickness. Remove the top piece of wax paper.

3. Place a texture block on top of the dough, texture side facing down, but don't press down yet. Use a knife to outline the block's perimeter in the dough and cut it out.

4. Cover the upholstery foam with wax paper and place it on a hard, flat surface. Place the cut piece of dough attached to the texture block on top of the covered foam. Push the texture block into the dough. The soft foam will compress, making for a better impression in the dough.

5. Lift up the block, which will likely be stuck to the dough. Carefully separate them and place the dough on the baking sheet. Use a toothpick to poke holes in the recessed areas of the embossed textures.

6. Preheat the oven to 250°F (120°C or gas mark ½). Emboss additional pieces of rolled-out dough with different textures until the baking sheet is full. Place in the oven.

7. After ten minutes, remove the dough from the oven and check for air pockets. Poke holes in any pockets with a toothpick, and use an oven mitt to gently press the block to release the air. Return dough to the oven. Repeat as needed for the next thirty minutes. Bake for sixty to seventy minutes, or until light brown and hard. Some of the blocks may appear to be slightly distorted, which is fine because you will use extra padding when printing with them. Remove when done and cool completely on the cooling rack.

8. Paint at least two layers of white glue (such as Mod Podge) or gel medium on both sides of the block to seal it and to strengthen the block.

MATERIALS

- 2 cups (240 g) all-purpose flour
- ½ cup (150 g) salt
- ¾ cup (175 ml) water
- large bowl
- dry and liquid measuring cups
- large spoon
- baking sheet lined with parchment paper
- cooling rack
- assorted texture blocks
- wax paper
- rolling pin
- ½" (1.3 cm) upholstery foam (at least the dimensions of your largest texture block)
- toothpick or wooden skewer
- oven mitt
- white glue (such as Mod Podge) or gel medium
- container and foam brush
- knife
- oven

Combine the baker's clay ingredients until they start to form into a dough.

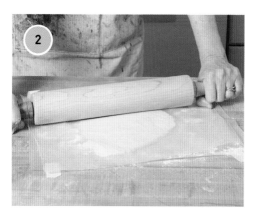

Sandwich the dough between sheets of wax paper and roll it out.

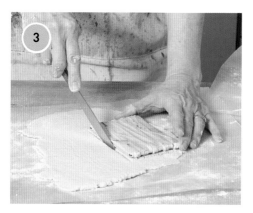

Place a texture block on top of the dough and use a knife to outline the block.

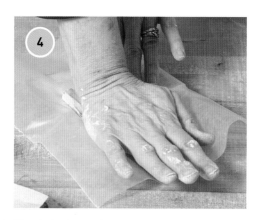

Place the dough-covered texture block on top of a piece of upholstery foam covered with wax paper and push down on it.

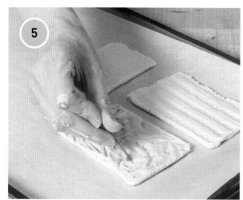

Separate the dough from the block and place it on a baking sheet.

Put the dough in the oven.

Bake until hard and let the blocks cool completely on a wire cooling rack

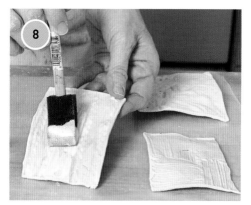

Seal with layers of white glue or gel medium.

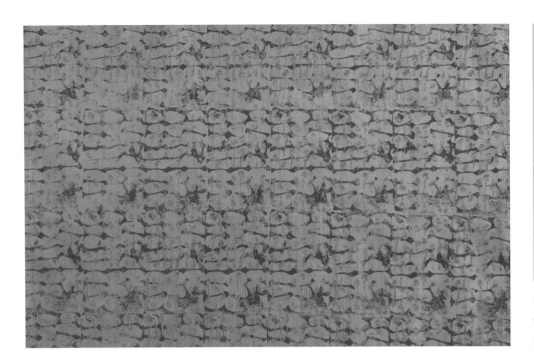

MATERIALS

- Basic Tool Kit (see page 13)
- 20" x 30" (51 x 76 cm) piece of ½" (1.3 cm) -thick upholstery foam (soft spongy foam, same type used for the daubers)
- 22" x 32" (56 x 81.5 cm) piece of muslin or cotton fabric
- cardboard blocks with kitchen staples and string
- embossed baker's clay blocks

Combine kitchen staple and baker's clay block prints in the same fabric to create a design with graphic tension between positive and negative patterns.

PRINTING WITH YOUR TEXTURE SQUARED BLOCKS

Now that you have a selection of both the "positive image" kitchen staple blocks and "negative image" embossed clay blocks, it's time to have some fun printing layers of textured fabric.

INSTRUCTIONS

1. Mix colors of opaque fabric paint or use colors directly from the bottles. If you are mixing a custom color, start with the lightest color and gradually add darker colors. Tape the edges of the fabric to your work surface. If you are printing with a more dimensional texture block or an embossed clay block, use extra padding under the fabric (see "Tip: Upholstery Foam for Dimensional Print Blocks" on page 43). Place the upholstery foam onto your portable work surface. Cover this with the muslin and tape your fabric to the muslin.

2. For print blocks made with flatter materials (such as spaghetti, toothpicks, or string), use a dense foam brayer to apply an even coat of paint. Spoon about ¼ teaspoon opaque fabric paint onto the glass palette. Roll the foam brayer back and forth until it is evenly coated with paint before rolling it over the block.

3. For blocks with more dimensional materials and for the embossed clay blocks, apply paint with a foam dauber.

4. Turn the paint-covered block onto the fabric and press to release the paint. Continue to apply paint and print with the first block to create the first texture layer on the fabric.

5. Use a baker's clay block to print a second layer to create a fabric rich with texture.

Use extra padding (½" [1.3 cm] upholstery foam) when printing with dimensional texture blocks.

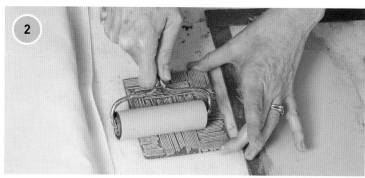

If you are using a block with flatter materials (such as spaghetti), use a paint-coated brayer to apply an even coat of paint to the block.

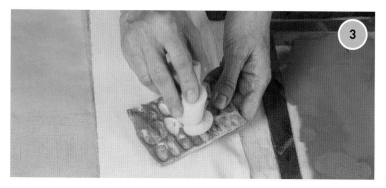

Use a foam dauber to apply fabric paint to the more dimensional embossed baker's clay block.

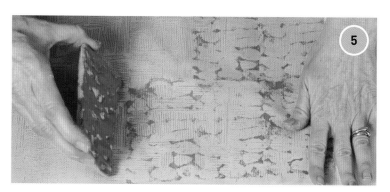

Press the block onto the fabric to release the paint.

Print a second layer with a baker's clay texture block to add depth to the fabric.

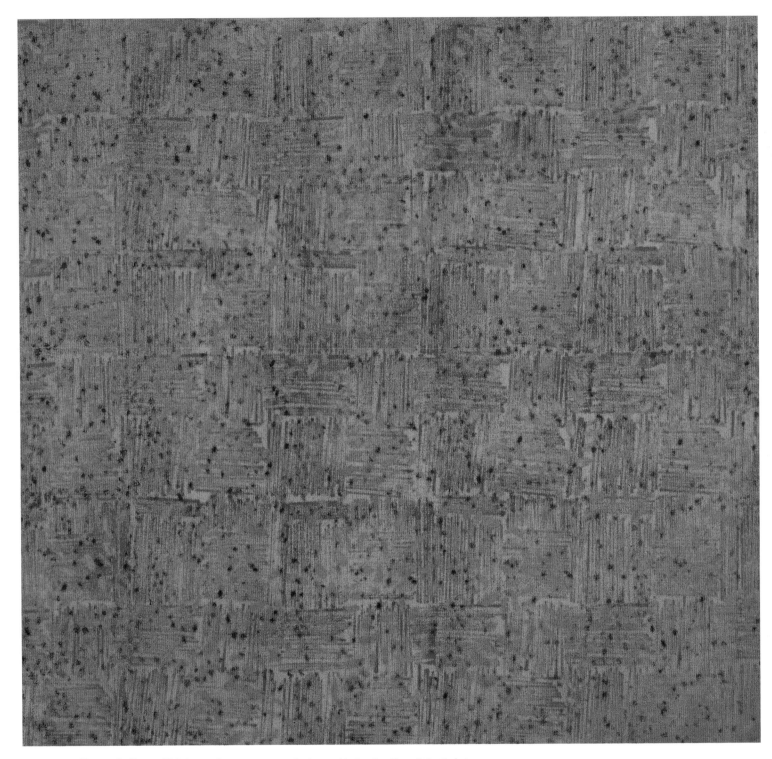

Print brayer rubbings to build up multiple layers of texture or use as a background texture for other printing techniques.

BRAYER RUBBINGS WITH THE BLOCKS

Brayer rubbings work best with cardboard texture blocks. Use the extra upholstery padding with this technique.

INSTRUCTIONS

1. Cover the portable work surface with the upholstery foam and muslin. Tape the edges of the fabric to this surface. Make sure you can easily slip the print block between the fabric and the muslin-covered upholstery foam.

2. Spoon about ¼ teaspoon opaque fabric paint onto the glass palette. Roll the foam brayer back and forth until it is evenly coated with paint.

3. Roll the paint across the fabric that is covering the block.

4. Carefully shift the block to a new location under the fabric and roll more paint across the fabric now covering the block. Continue until you cover the entire piece of fabric.

MATERIALS

- Basic Toolkit (see page 13)
- 20" x 30" (51 x 76 cm) piece of ½" (1.3 cm) -thick upholstery foam
- 22" x 32" (56 x 81.5 cm) piece of muslin or cotton fabric
- cardboard blocks with kitchen staples and string

TIP: Upholstery Foam for Dimensional Print Blocks

Use upholstery foam for better prints. Kitchen staple blocks with dimensional materials such as beans and almonds and embossed blocks will print better with a cushion of ½" (1.3 cm) soft upholstery foam. The soft foam will compress as the paint-covered block is pushed into it. More parts of the block will make contact with the fabric. Use the upholstery foam for brayer rubbings as well.

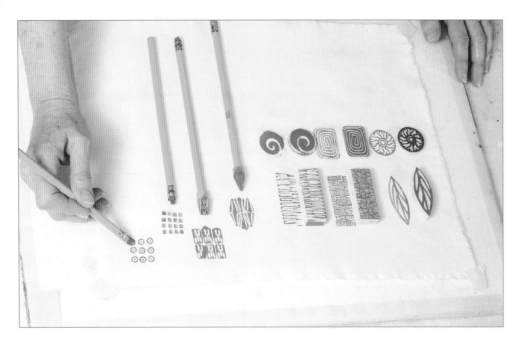

MATERIALS

- linoleum cutters with #1 and #2 tips
- craft knife
- pencils for eraser carving and drawing
- triangular pencil top erasers
- flat erasers: rectangular and other shapes
- optional: tracing paper and plastic spoon

Print your fabric with different sizes of carved erasers to add tiny details or to repeat patterns, textures, or small motifs.

Found Objects and Kitchen Tools

Oh the possibilities! I'm ready to show you how to tackle designing and printing fabrics with the items in the kitchen catchall drawer, the week's recycling, and the local dollar store.

With so many choices, I decided to group items by size and type. I created some "inventory prints" and considered how I would combine and layer prints with these objects and tools. In the end, I designed a nine-patch square using small scale items from my kitchen catchall drawer. You could also design a fabric featuring larger scale patterns and textures printed with kitchen tools.

ERASER FUN

I love carving stamp designs! You might be used to working with larger blocks, but you can still carve and cut a variety of designs from flat, shaped erasers, triangular pencil top erasers, and even the erasers on pencils. Remember that the areas carved away will not print, while the areas that remain will print.

Pencil Erasers

Although a pencil eraser is the smallest type of eraser, it still offers a variety of options. Use the #1 tip in your linoleum cutter to carve tiny designs such as concentric circles, a cross, a star, or a spiral. Use a craft knife to cut simple shapes such as a square or triangle. These stamps can add tiny details to your fabric designs.

Triangular pencil top erasers are very versatile for printing, offering a variety of shapes including the linear tip, circular bottom, flat rectangular side, and triangular side. Both the flat rectangular and triangular sides can be carved with a linoleum cutter. Carve simple designs such as lines, circles, or spirals. Alternate printing the eraser in up and down positions for interesting textural effects.

Shaped Erasers: Carving Textures and Designs

These are the largest of the erasers and give you the best opportunity to design detailed stamps. You can freehand carve simple texture designs such as lines, cross hatches, spirals, or circles using the #1 or #2 linoleum cutter tips. For a more detailed design or image, use tracing paper. Trace around the shape of the eraser, draw a design (or trace one) inside the shape with a pencil, turn the traced design back over onto the eraser, and rub the back of the paper with the back of a plastic spoon to transfer the design. Don't carve the pencil lines; instead carve the areas between the lines. If you only have access to the standard rectangular erasers, you can cut them into shapes using a craft knife. Combine rectangular texture stamps with shaped design stamps for a more complex fabric design.

Shaped erasers are easy to carve and offer lots of design possibilities.

HELPFUL HINT

Take a careful look at your found object. Can you print with the top, bottom, or sides of it? Can you roll it? Is one part of it more visually interesting than another?

To create interesting printed patterns and make found object printing go more quickly, band together multiples of the same item (see photo). This works well with pencils and corks. To print a design with thumbtacks, push them into layers of corrugated cardboard. This makes applying the fabric paint much easier and printing a bit safer!

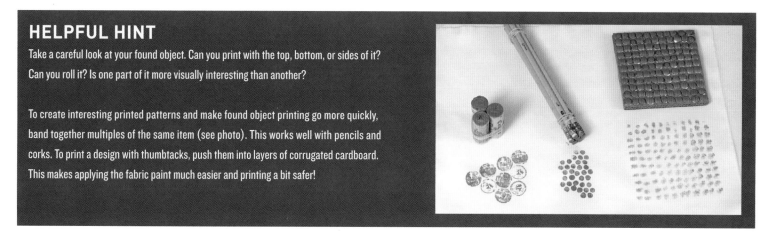

MATERIALS

- Basic Tool Kit (see page 13)
- small-scale items for printing, including pens, pencils, markers, pencil grips, shaped and pencil top erasers, thumbtacks, corks, small bottle caps
- disappearing or water-soluble marker
- clear plastic gridded ruler
- blue painter's tape
- push pins

I built up complex patterns using everyday objects from my "catchall" drawer, including pencils, erasers, pencil grips, and pen tops.

Small Scale Items: Nine-Patch

I enjoy designing fabrics with multiple layers of printing and repeating visual elements. Looking at the inventory prints of my small-scale found objects, I saw circles everywhere: pencil erasers, pen caps, the ends of pencil grips, thumbtacks, and bottle corks. I knew that this shape would play a major role in designing this piece.

I opted for a nine-patch design to show off prints created with these smaller items. Although the format is traditional, it's the optical effects of the predominately circular small-scale designs within the patches that give it a more modern vibe.

To add a textural element to some of the squares, I cut and carved shaped and pencil top erasers and rolled paint-covered pencils and pencil grips across the fabric.

This piece of fabric took multiple hours to complete because many of the shapes were printed one at a time. To save some printing time, see "Helpful Hint" on page 45. Consider using fabrics made with these found objects for smaller home décor projects and personal items such as pillows, book or journal covers, small purses, wallets, or eyeglass cases.

INSTRUCTIONS

1. Tape the fabric to your work surface. Use a disappearing or water-soluble marker and a ruler to measure and mark the nine-patch design. If you are planning multiple printing sessions, use the water-soluble marker, because it will remain on the fabric until you wash it out. (See A.)

2. Mix up a selection of opaque fabric paint colors or use colors directly from the bottles. I suggest choosing two to three base colors and then mixing some tints of those colors. Select and mask off one square at a time using the blue painter's tape. (See B.)

3. Refer to your inventory of found objects and pattern samplers for design ideas. Consider printing a background texture with carved erasers or rolling a paint-covered pencil, pencil grips, or cork across the masked off square. For easier printing, slide one or two pencil grips onto a pencil. Stick push pins into the ends of the cork. Use a foam brayer to apply paint to the flat carved eraser and a dauber or foam brush to apply paint to the pencil, grips, and cork.

4. Print patterns with small-scale found objects. I used the ends of pencil grips, the circular end of a pencil top eraser, and carved pencil top erasers. Use a foam dauber to apply paint. Print designs using items that are banded together, such as pencils or corks. Add more details with pencil erasers (some carved, others plain), thumbtacks, marker caps, and so on. (See C.)

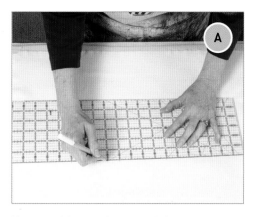

Measure and draw out the nine-patch design with a water-soluble marker.

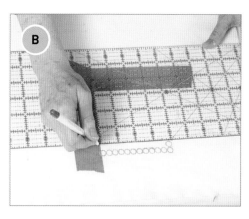

Use blue painter's tape to mask off each square before printing.

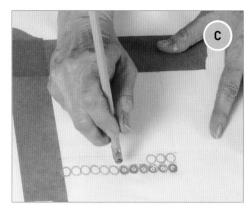

Add details to the design to build up complex patterns.

beyond the potato print:
USING VEGETABLES AND FRUIT TO CREATE FABRIC DESIGNS

was recently inspired to take a fresh look at printing with vegetables and fruit. Two months after I visited a good friend and sampled the delicious vegetables from her husband's garden, she mentioned that they were eating fresh sweet corn right off the cob. "I wonder about corncob printing," she said. "Maybe even a fruits-of-the-summer theme."

I wondered about corncob printing, too. I approached my next trip to the produce section with wide eyes and an open mind. Everywhere I looked, I saw the potential for designing playful, colorful fabrics using the shapes and textures of vegetables and fruit in unexpected ways.

In this chapter, you will learn how to create textured backgrounds by printing directly with vegetables and how to turn root vegetables such as carrots, turnips, and radishes into carved print blocks. You will cut and print with shaped vegetable slices and learn how to make nature prints and brayer rubbings with leafy lettuces and herbs. Discover how to design "fresh" fabrics with backgrounds and shapes directly inspired by your garden or market.

Print textures on fabric with corn, broccoli, carrot slices, and greens. Overprint with carved radishes to design a "juicy" fabric, such as the one opposite.

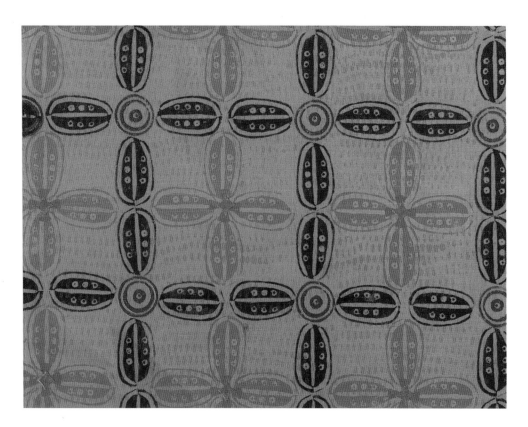

MATERIALS

- Basic Tool Kit (see page 13)
- paring knife
- cutting board for cutting vegetables
- assorted textural vegetables (such as broccoli, corn on the cob, cabbage, cauliflower, onions, and Brussels sprouts)
- corn holders to stick onto the ends of corn on the cob so it can be rolled across the fabric more easily (optional but recommended)

The printed background texture is created by rolling paint-covered corn on the cob across the fabric. The design is printed with carved radishes and carrots.

Creating Background Textures with Vegetables

Often when I design fabrics, I like to start by printing a textured background. When printing with vegetables, this means choosing those that either have obvious textural parts, such as broccoli, or those that must be cut in half to expose the textured layers, as in the case of cabbage or onions. Here are the basic steps for applying fabric paint and printing background textures with three vegetables: broccoli, cabbage, and corn on the cob.

INSTRUCTIONS

1. Tape the edges of the fabric to your portable work surface.

2. Prepare the vegetables. Shuck and clean the corn and put a corn holder on each end; break off pieces of the broccoli. Use a paring knife to cut the cabbage in half to expose its textured layers.

3. Mix up colors of opaque fabric paint or use colors directly from the bottles. If you are mixing a custom color, start with the lightest color and gradually add darker colors. Spoon about ¼ teaspoon paint onto a glass palette.

4. Use a foam dauber (see "How to Make a Foam Dauber" on page 21) to pick up some of the paint. You may want to daub the paint on the palette a few times if you pick up too much paint at first. (See A.)

5. Use the paint-covered dauber to apply the paint to the vegetable. For certain textured vegetables, such as corn on the cob, it's easier and faster to apply paint with a foam brush. Dip the brush into the container of paint and brush it across the edge of the container to release excess paint before applying it to the corn. (See B.)

A

Use a foam dauber to apply paint to textured vegetables such as broccoli.

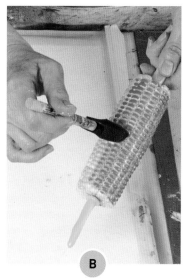

B

Brush paint onto corn on the cob.

C

Press the paint-covered broccoli onto the fabric to release the paint.

D

Roll the paint-covered corn across the fabric.

6. In the case of the paint-covered broccoli and cabbage, turn the vegetable over onto the fabric and press. Broccoli texture prints, for example, make a great background. You can overprint this texture with carved vegetable designs. (See C.)

7. For the paint-covered corn on the cob, hold on to the ends of the corn (or use corn holders) and roll the cob across the fabric. The printed textures will appear darker at the start and fade as the corn is rolled across the fabric. Apply more paint to the corn to roll over the lighter areas or roll in different directions for additional texture. (See D.)

8. Reapply fabric paint as needed. Consider using different layers of colors for more interest (see "Making Marbled Fabric with Cabbage Prints" on page 53).

TIP: Mixing and Using Paint

If you are printing on a colored fabric, consider mixing a color that is slightly lighter (by adding white) or slightly darker (by adding black or gray) than the fabric color. You can also experiment with making the color slightly warmer (by adding a warm color such as yellow or red) or slightly cooler (by adding a cool color such as blue) or mixing in a little bit of the complementary color (e.g., red into green). These suggested color mixtures will additionally help the vegetable prints to read as background texture.

If you printed your vegetable textures on white fabric, you can hand-paint a background color over the textures using diluted transparent fabric paint (see "Painting Fabric Backgrounds with Transparent Fabric Paints" on page 16). Choose a color that blends well or enhances the texture prints.

Overlapping prints made with a cabbage gives the impression of marbled fabric.

Making Marbled Fabric with Cabbage Prints

Printing with cabbage can mimic the look of marbled fabric. You will need:

- a fat quarter piece of either hand-painted or solid color commercial fabric
- a head of cabbage cut in half
- three different colors of opaque fabric paint, with at least one color contrasting with the color of the fabric (see "Tip: Mixing and Using Paint" on page 51)
- a foam dauber for each paint color

INSTRUCTIONS

1. Choose your first paint color and apply it to one of the cabbage halves with a foam dauber.

2. Turn the cabbage half over onto the fabric and press to release the paint. Reapply the same color paint and print again with the cabbage. Continue to reapply paint to the cabbage before each print. Scatter your prints over the fat quarter, leaving some areas unprinted.

3. Let the fabric paint dry.

4. Apply a different color to either the same or another cabbage half and print. These prints should overlay some of the prints made with the previous color.

5. After the second paint color is dry, continue with the third color. Stop printing when you are happy with the overlaying designs on the fabric.

CARROTS THREE WAYS

Try carving or cutting designs in carrots in three different ways.

1. Use a paring or craft knife to cut off the top of the carrot so you have a smooth, flat, circular surface. Cut or carve a small design.

2. Slice the carrot lengthwise. Use your linoleum carving tool to carve a simple design. One suggestion is to carve along either side of the center of the root and then cut shorter lines across.

3. Cut a cylindrical section out of a whole carrot, making sure it has the same diameter all the way around. Peel the carrot to provide a smooth surface. Carve designs into the carrot. Insert corn holders into each end of the carrot cylinder. After applying paint with a foam dauber, roll it across the fabric to transfer the design.

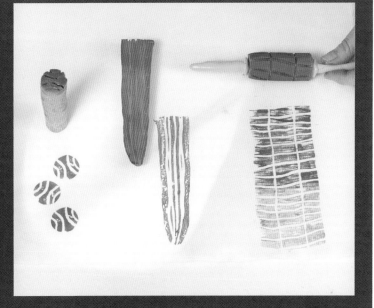

Carrots are a versatile vegetable! Carve designs in a circular cross section, along the length of a cut carrot or make a number of designs around a cylindrical section.

This simple, yet bold design uses a carved turnip and a slice of green pepper.

Carving Print Blocks from Vegetables

Many people's first printing experience was to cut a design in a potato half, turn it over onto a stamp pad or apply paint with a brush, and press the design onto a piece of paper. These simple prints are a lovely way to create designs on fabric. With that thought in mind, I decided to explore the produce section of my local market to see what other vegetables might lend themselves to cut or carved designs.

It turns out that there is a whole group of vegetables that fit the bill quite nicely—root vegetables, such as carrots, radishes, turnips, parsnips, rutabagas, and yams. I decided to experiment with carrots, radishes, and turnips, as they are readily available and easy to cut and carve. These vegetables offer a variety of sizes and shapes that when carved and printed together can produce an endless variety of playful fabric designs.

INSTRUCTIONS

1. Tape the edges of the fabric to your portable work surface.

2. Prepare the vegetables. Cut them in half, or in the case of a large turnip, cut it in thirds. You will want enough surface area and depth in each cut section to cut a design with a knife or carve one with linoleum carving tools. After cutting the vegetables, turn them over cut side down onto a doubled layer of paper towel to absorb excess moisture. (See A.)

3. The linoleum carving tool consists of a handle and a set of different-size carving tips. Choose either the #2 or #3 tip and insert it into the handle. Hold the tool at a comfortable angle and press the edge of the tip into the flesh of the vegetable. While holding the vegetable steady with the other hand, carve a design. (You can also use other tools or objects such as a ballpoint pen, fork, wooden skewer, and so on, to poke holes or impress designs into the vegetable.) (See B.)

4. Mix up colors of opaque paint or use colors directly from the bottles. If you are mixing a custom color, start with the lightest color and gradually add darker colors.

Cut root vegetables, such as a radish, in half to expose a flat surface for carving designs.

Use a linoleum carving tool to carve simple designs.

Print multiples of one carved vegetable design or combine two or more together to build up bold patterns.

5. Use your foam dauber to pick up some of the paint. Daub the paint on the palette a few times if you pick up too much at first.

6. Use the paint-covered dauber to apply paint to the carved or cut vegetable design.

7. Turn the paint-covered vegetable over onto the fabric and press to release the paint. Reapply paint before each print. (See C.)

HELPFUL HINT:
Create a Printed Sampler

Before printing your final fat quarter fabrics with your carved and cut root vegetables, try creating a printed sampler. Choose one color and print all of your vegetable blocks. In this way, you can see which ones may work well together to create a more complex design.

Printing a sampler is a helpful way to see all your vegetable print block options.

MATERIALS

- Basic Tool Kit (see page 13)
- paring knife
- cutting board
- cookie cutters
- craft knife (optional but recommended)
- assorted vegetables (such as carrots, radishes, turnips, potatoes, yams, green peppers, squash, and cucumbers)

Use cookie cutters to cut out shapes from slices of vegetables. You can then carve designs into the shapes for more interest.

Slicing and Dicing: Printing with Vegetable Shapes

Some vegetables can be sliced into thin sections that can then be cut into shapes and printed. The resulting prints will display some of the textural qualities of the vegetables used. You can cut shapes with a craft knife or metal cookie cutters.

INSTRUCTIONS

1. Tape the edges of the fabric to your portable work surface. Prepare the vegetables. Cut ¼" (6 mm) cross sections of vegetables such as turnips, or cut lengthwise sections of vegetables such as zucchini. Cut apart a green (or other sweet) pepper. Use a craft knife or metal cookie cutters to cut simple shapes. After cutting out the vegetable shapes, place them on a doubled layer of paper towel. Let the paper towel absorb some of the excess moisture before applying paint. (See A.)

2. Mix up colors of opaque fabric paint or use colors directly from the bottles. If you are mixing a custom color, start with the lightest color and gradually add darker colors.

3. Once the excess moisture has been wicked away by the paper towel, apply the paint to the vegetable using your foam dauber. Turn the shape over onto the fabric and press to release the paint. (See B.)

PERFECT PARING: Printing with Fruit

The unique and distinctive shapes of fruit are perfect for fabric printing. Some fruits, such as citrus and star fruits, are too juicy to be carved but can be used for printing with a cross section for interesting geometric designs. Other fruits, such as apples and pears (unripe ones are best), can be sliced in half and carved to add a bit of whimsy to their recognizable forms. Slices of smooth melon and citrus fruit rinds can also be carved, while the rough rind of the cantaloupe makes a wonderful textural impression on fabric.

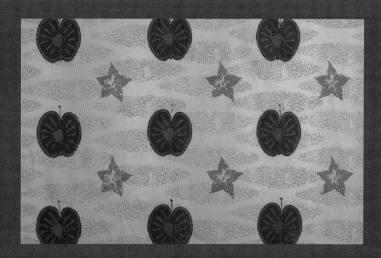

A carved apple half and a slice of star fruit create this cheery design. The background texture is printed with cantaloupe rind.

(A)

Using cookie cutters is an easy and fun way to create shaped print blocks from vegetables.

(B)

Press the painted vegetable onto the fabric.

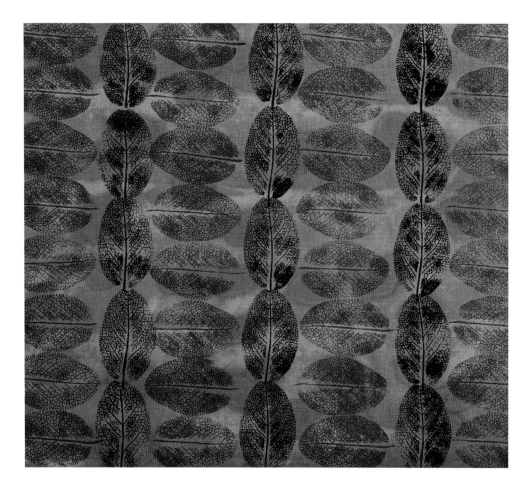

The delicate details of this sage leaf are captured by directly applying paint with a foam dauber.

- Basic Tool Kit (see page 13)
- assorted leafy vegetables and herbs (such as lettuces, kale, spinach, sage, and mint)

Lovely Leaves

Leafy vegetables and wide-leaf herbs lend themselves to direct printing as well as being placed under the fabric for brayer rubbings.

INSTRUCTIONS

1. Tape the edges of the fabric to your portable work surface. Sandwich wet leaves between paper towels to soak up extra moisture before applying paint.

2. Mix up colors of opaque fabric paint or use colors directly from the bottles. If you are mixing a custom color, start with the lightest color and gradually add darker colors.

3. There are two different methods for applying paint to the leaves for direct printing. In both cases, apply the paint to the back side of the leaf, which will be the more textured side.
- Apply with a dauber, taking care to apply an even layer of paint across the entire leaf. When applying paint to herbs, use this technique.

- Apply with a foam brayer. Place ¼ teaspoon paint onto the glass palette and roll the foam brayer back and forth to spread the paint until it evenly coats the brayer. Roll an even layer of paint over the leaf.

4. Place the leaf, paint side down, on the fabric. Cover with a paper towel and press to release the paint. For additional prints, reapply the paint.

MATERIALS
- Basic Tool Kit (see page 13)
- assorted leafy vegetables and herbs (such as lettuces, kale, spinach, sage, and mint)

Soft leaf impressions can be obtained with a brayer rubbing.

Brayer Rubbings

With brayer rubbings, no paint is applied directly to the leaf or vegetable. Instead the leaf or vegetable is placed under the fabric and a thin layer of paint is rolled across the fabric that covers it. (See "Three Printing Techniques" on page 30 for more on brayer rubbings.)

INSTRUCTIONS

1. Tape the edges of the fabric to your portable work surface and slip a leaf or leaves under the fabric.

2. Spoon about ¼ teaspoon paint onto the glass palette and roll the foam brayer back and forth to spread the paint until it evenly coats the brayer.

3. Roll the paint-covered brayer across the fabric. Use just enough pressure when rolling the paint across the fabric to pick up the texture of the leaves underneath.

4. Adjust the positioning of the leaves to continue.

CHAPTER 4

wrap it up!
WRAPS AND FOIL

When working with new materials, it's important to have a playful, open attitude and time in the studio. These two things go hand-in-hand. Tactile acts such as tearing, cutting, folding, and wrapping can inspire you and get you in the mood to explore.

When I'm experimenting, I'm reminded of projects I did when I was young. Working with wax paper immediately brings back memories of gathering red and orange maple leaves and having Mom iron them between the translucent sheets. I can still imagine them glowing in the window. This vivid memory had me pondering, "What if I sealed herb leaves and other small items in wax paper—could I print with this 'sandwich'?"

In this chapter, you will learn how to turn those rolls of wraps into printing plates, stencils, and masks. You'll wrap plastic wrap around the ends of cardboard tubes and over margarine tubs to turn them into tools to monoprint whimsical fabrics with dots and swirls. You'll discover how to emboss aluminum foil to create decorative folk art fabrics. Enjoy exploring all the creative fabric design possibilities "wrapped up" in these products we use every day.

Freezer paper is a versatile paper product and a great surface design tool. Tear it to create organic shapes or cut detailed stencils such as the cats in the image opposite, inspired by layered appliqué designs called *molas*.

Freezer Paper Fun:
Masks and Stencils

Freezer paper is an amazingly versatile, inexpensive, and easy-to-work-with product that you will come back to again and again. The key to its versatility is its two sides: an uncoated paper side and a plastic-coated side. Quilters and home sewers find it ideal for creating templates for appliqué and clothing patterns. By heating the plastic-coated side with an iron, it can be attached to fabric. For fabric designs, tear or cut it and iron it to fabric to mask off areas. It can also be turned into sturdy stencils. Apply paint in different ways to freezer paper masks and stencils to get a range of effects from watercolor backgrounds to intricate prints.

FREEZER PAPER MASK DESIGNS

Here are three ways to make freezer paper mask designs. Each technique offers unique surface design effects when combined with different paint applications. After creating the designs, carefully iron them, using the cotton setting on your iron, with the plastic coating facing the fabric. The heat will warm up the plastic-coated side so it sticks to the fabric.

Tear Designs. Tear a piece of freezer paper from the roll. Carefully tear designs out of the paper. These can be amorphous shapes or simple designs such as circles, spirals, hearts, or strips. (See A.)

Fold-and-Scissor-Cut Designs. Remember making paper snowflakes? That is the idea behind this technique. With the uncoated paper side facing out, fold the freezer paper in different ways and then cut out designs with your scissors. (See B.)

Craft Knife-Cut Designs. For cutting detailed designs, a craft knife works best. Tape a piece of freezer paper to a cutting mat with the uncoated paper side facing up. Draw designs on the paper to cut away or cut freehand. The openings cut from the mask will expose the fabric to the paint. (See C.)

MATERIALS

- freezer paper (such as Reynolds freezer paper)
- scissors
- craft knife
- self-healing cutting mat
- clear plastic gridded ruler
- #2 pencil
- masking tape
- iron and ironing board
- pressing cloth (such as cotton or muslin fabric)

Tear freezer paper into any kind of shape, such as strips, shown here.

Create a mask design by folding and scissor cutting freezer paper.

Use a craft knife to cut detailed designs before ironing the freezer paper mask to your fabric.

HELPFUL HINT: Mask versus Stencil

What is the difference between a mask and a stencil? Is there an advantage to using one or the other? A mask is material applied directly to the fabric to protect certain areas from receiving the application of fabric paint. A stencil is also made from material that covers some areas and exposes other areas of the fabric to paint. Because masks are applied directly to the fabric, they are usually used only once (although a freezer paper mask can often be used again if there is still plastic coating on the paper). Stencils are made of stiffer materials that can be picked up and moved to another area of the fabric for printing repeats of the same design.

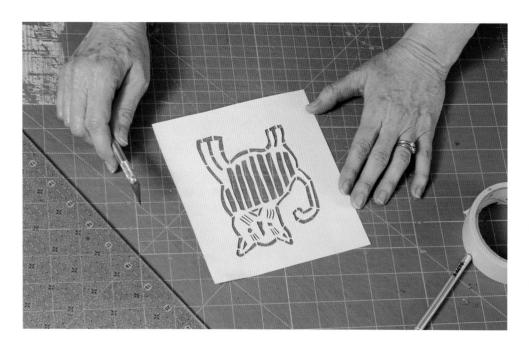

- two pieces of freezer paper cut to the same size
- a piece of paper for a stencil design (optional)
- craft knife
- self-healing cutting mat
- clear plastic gridded ruler
- #2 pencil
- masking tape
- iron and ironing board
- pressing cloth (such as cotton or muslin)

Cut out bold designs from two sheets of freezer paper ironed together to form a sturdy stencil.

FREEZER PAPER STENCILS

To create a sturdy stencil, iron two sheets of freezer paper to each other. Use your craft knife to cut detailed designs out of the ironed paper. When doing this project, start with simple designs.

INSTRUCTIONS

1. Tape the drawing you wish to turn into a stencil to the cutting mat. Tape a single sheet of freezer paper, with the uncoated side facing up, over the drawing.

2. Use a pencil to trace the drawing or design directly on the single sheet of freezer paper, which is translucent. Even simple designs may need "bridges" to keep separate parts of the stencil together as one piece. Bridges are small connections (often in the form of strips) that bridge the gap between sections of the stencil. Add them to your design with a pencil before cutting.

3. Iron the freezer paper design to the second piece of freezer paper with the plastic-coated sides together. Cover the freezer paper with the pressing cloth to protect the iron. Iron from the center of the design out to the edges to avoid wrinkles and air pockets.

4. Carefully cut out the design using a craft knife. If you accidently cut through a bridge, create a new one with a small piece of masking tape. Remember that the fabric paint will go through the openings of the stencil to create the design on the fabric.

TIP: Bold Is Best

For stencil design ideas, look at books with decorative patterns or bold motifs from other cultures. Designs with strong contrasts (black and white are best) will be easiest to turn into stencils.

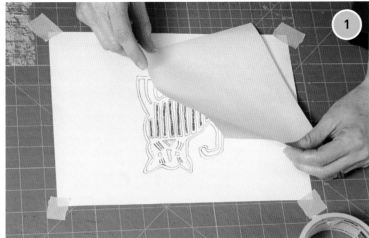

Tape freezer paper over the drawing you wish to turn into a stencil design.

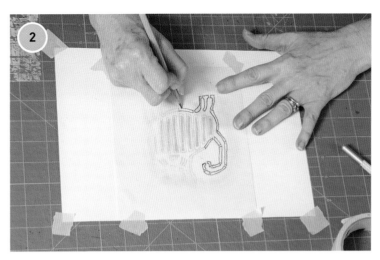

Pencil in "bridges" as you work out the stencil design. These small connections help hold the parts of the stencil together.

Iron a second, backing sheet of freezer paper to the drawn stencil design. This double layer of freezer paper will create a sturdy stencil.

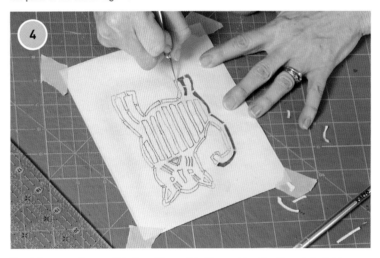

Carefully cut out the stencil design with a craft knife—avoid cutting through the bridges.

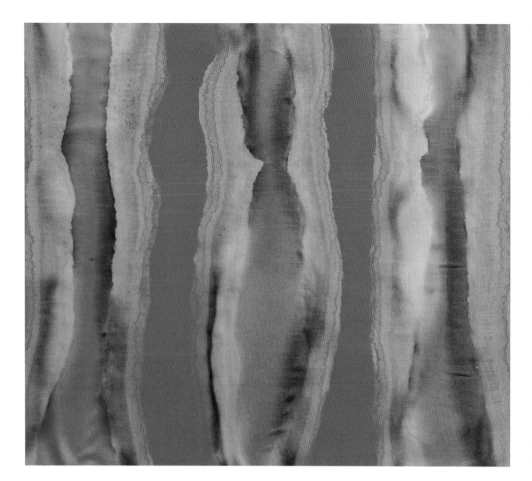

MATERIALS

- Basic Tool Kit (see page 13)
- white or light-colored cotton fabric with torn freezer paper masks ironed to it

Paint over torn freezer paper masks for the look of water-color washes. Use two paint colors to achieve beautiful color blends from paint seeping under the freezer paper.

HOW TO APPLY PAINT TO FREEZER PAPER MASKS AND STENCILS

Apply fabric paints to freezer paper masks and stencils for surface design effects that range from watercolor washes to the look of soft pastel drawings. Have foam brushes, daubers, and dense foam brayers available for applying paint for the different techniques below.

Watercolor Effects

Use white or light-colored background fabric for this "wet" paint application technique.

Paint over torn freezer paper masks for the best results. The paint seeps under the freezer paper to create soft, watercolor effects with edges in the shapes of the torn designs. Fabrics made with this technique make great backgrounds for most of the techniques in this book.

INSTRUCTIONS

1. Tape the fabric with the ironed, torn freezer paper designs to your work surface.

2. Mix up two different colors of transparent fabric paint using the ratio of one part paint to two parts water. You can use the colors right from the container or mix a custom color. If you choose to mix a custom color, start with the lightest color and mix in the darker color(s) a little at a time. Add the water after mixing your desired color.

3. Apply the paints with foam brushes.

4. Let the paint dry completely before removing the freezer paper masks.

Pastel Effects

Roll a paint-covered dense foam brayer over torn or scissor-cut freezer paper masks to achieve the look of soft pastel drawings.

INSTRUCTIONS

1. Tape the fabric with freezer paper designs to your work surface. Use opaque fabric paint colors directly from the bottles or mix custom colors.

2. Spoon about ¼ teaspoon opaque fabric paint onto a glass palette. Roll a dense foam brayer back and forth until it is evenly coated with paint.

To achieve the look of soft pastel drawings, roll a paint-covered brayer over torn or cut freezer paper shapes.

3. Roll the paint-covered brayer over the freezer paper masks. You may have to roll in different directions or try different amounts of pressure on the brayer to get the best results.

4. Let the paint dry completely before removing the freezer paper masks.

Dauber for Details

Applying paint with a foam dauber works well with all types of freezer paper masks and is the best application technique to use with intricate designs (both mask and stencil) cut with a craft knife.

INSTRUCTIONS

1. Tape the fabric with attached freezer paper masks to your work surface or, if you plan to use a freezer paper stencil, tape it to the fabric. Use opaque fabric paint colors directly from the bottles or mix custom colors.

2. Spoon about ¼ teaspoon opaque fabric paint onto a glass palette.

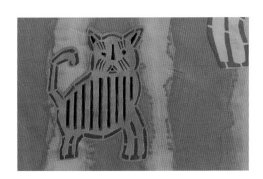

Use foam daubers to apply paint through detailed freezer paper stencil designs.

3. Pick up some paint with a foam dauber. Press it against the glass to release any excess paint.

4. Daub the paint along the edges of the freezer paper masks and across mask or stencil design details. Pick up more paint

with the dauber as needed or change paint colors as desired.

5. Let the paint dry completely before removing the freezer paper masks or leave the masks attached to the fabric to add more texture and design details. Reposition stencils as desired.

Print whimsical fabric designs with plastic containers and cardboard tubes covered with plastic wrap.

MATERIALS

- Basic Tool Kit (see page 13)
- 20" x 30" (51 x 76 cm) piece of ½" (1.3 cm) -thick upholstery foam
- 22" x 32" (56 x 81.5 cm) piece of muslin or cotton fabric
- plastic containers, cups, and cardboard tubes of different diameters
- plastic wrap
- rubber bands
- small bristle brushes for detailed designs
- undiluted or slightly diluted (1:1 paint:water ratio) transparent fabric paint

Playing with Plastic Wrap

When discoveries happen in the studio, it's always exciting. While looking about for a vehicle for printing with plastic wrap, I couldn't help but see the answer staring me in the face. On my printing table I have an assortment of margarine and yogurt containers, plastic cups, cardboard tubes, and rubber bands. Plastic wrap is used to cover containers of food, I thought. Why not cover these items with plastic wrap, secure the wrap with rubber bands, and use them to print? Hours of printing-play ensued! I had so much fun with this printing technique that I can't wait to try it again!

INSTRUCTIONS

1. Tear or cut the plastic wrap to fit over the plastic containers, cups, or the circular ends of the cardboard tubes.

2. Secure the wrap with rubber bands. Make sure that the plastic wrap is smooth and taut.

3. Add extra padding to your work surface for better prints by placing the upholstery foam onto it. Cover the foam with the piece of muslin or cotton and then tape your fabric to it.

4. Paint designs on the flat, circular surfaces of the plastic-wrapped containers and tubes. The designs can cover the entire circular surface (this works especially well with the cardboard tubes) or paint textures and design details on just part of the plastic surface.

5. Press onto the fabric to release the paint.

6. Layer prints and colors to create whimsical fabrics.

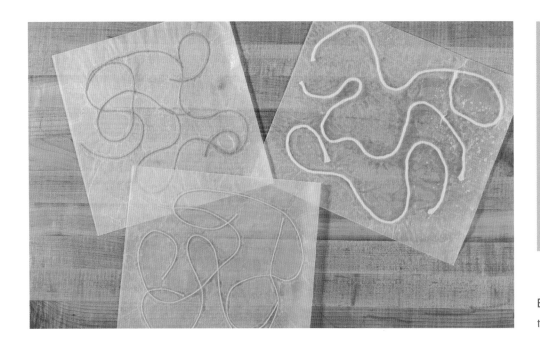

MATERIALS

- wax paper
- scissors
- fresh herbs with textured leaves (such as sage or mint)
- string or twine of different thicknesses
- other small, flat items (such as paperclips and thin rubber bands)
- iron and ironing board
- pressing cloth (such as cotton or muslin)

Encase flat household items, such as string, between two sheets of wax paper to create a printing plate.

The Wonders of Wax Paper

Inspired by childhood memories of jewel-toned autumn leaves captured between sheets of ironed wax paper, I used the same technique to create wax paper printing plates. Arrange textured herb leaves, bits of string, paper clips, or other flat items between two sheets of wax paper. Seal your designs with an iron and you are ready to start printing!

CREATING A WAX PAPER PRINTING PLATE

Arrange groupings or patterns of flat objects between wax paper sheets before sealing with an iron. When you print with these printing plates, you can quickly and easily create patterned fabric designs.

INSTRUCTIONS

1. Tear or cut two pieces of wax paper from a roll.

2. Arrange items such as fresh herbs, string, or paper clips on one of the pieces.

3. Cover the items with the second piece of wax paper.

4. Cover with a pressing cloth and use a hot iron to melt the coating on the paper to encase the items.

TIP: Press, Seal, Print!

Press-and-seal wraps are an easy alternative to working with wax paper. Place items between two pieces of the wrap and press the area around them for a tight seal, smoothing around the contours of the items. No ironing required!

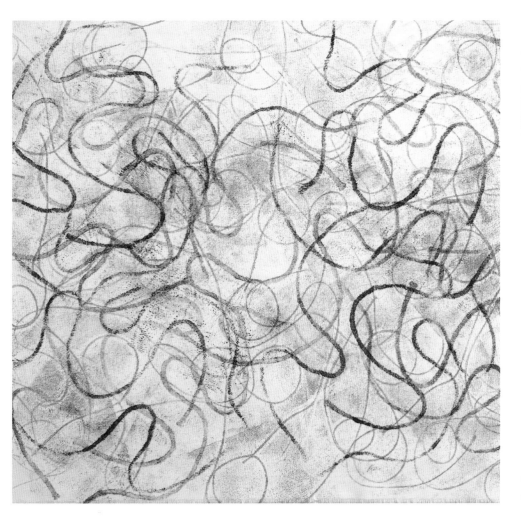

MATERIALS
- Basic Tool Kit (see page 13)
- undiluted transparent fabric paint
- an additional dense foam brayer

Make a number of wax paper printing plates using different weights of string. Layer prints to create a fabric with lots of energy and movement.

PRINTING WITH THE WAX PAPER PRINTING PLATE

Use wax paper printing plates to print multiple images quickly. Create a richly layered fabric by printing with a number of plates that encase different or related items.

INSTRUCTIONS

1. Tape the edges of the fabric to your work surface.

2. Use undiluted transparent fabric paint directly from the bottles or mix custom colors. Undiluted transparent fabric paint does not dry as quickly as opaque paint on the wax paper and tends to pick up more details in the printing plate.

3. Spoon ¼ teaspoon undiluted transparent fabric paint onto a glass palette. Roll a dense foam brayer back and forth until it is evenly coated with paint.

4. Roll the painted-covered brayer across the items sealed in the wax paper printing plate.

5. Turn the printing plate onto the fabric and roll a clean dense foam brayer across the back side of it to release the paint. Carefully lift the printing plate off the fabric.

MATERIALS

- 18" (45.5 cm) -wide heavy-duty aluminum foil
- clear plastic gridded ruler
- permanent marker
- scissors
- tools for embossing foil (such as a ballpoint pen, pencil, or wooden end of a small paintbrush)
- tracing paper (optional)

Design decorative fabrics with folk art–inspired motifs by painting and printing embossed aluminum foil printing plates.

Folk Art Foil: Embossed Designs in Aluminum Foil

I often look at folk art and craft traditions for fabric design inspiration. As I considered how to print with aluminum foil, I couldn't help but think about Mexican tin art. Recycled tin is embossed and painted with whimsical folk art designs. Embossing creates a contrast of raised and recessed areas—just what is needed for printing!

Fold heavy-duty aluminum foil and emboss with a ballpoint pen, pencil, or the wooden end of a small paintbrush. I just started doodling in the foil with these tools and came up with a bold folk art–inspired flower design. Brush or roll transparent fabric paint on this printing plate. Either side can be used, yielding subtly different results. You will need to occasionally "refresh" the design by going over it with one of the embossing tools. This can be an opportunity to add more

or different details. Design fabrics for pillows or curtain panels using this technique.

DESIGN AN EMBOSSED FOIL PRINTING PLATE

Embossed foil printing plates are easy to make and a great way to create unique fabric designs with a folk art flair.

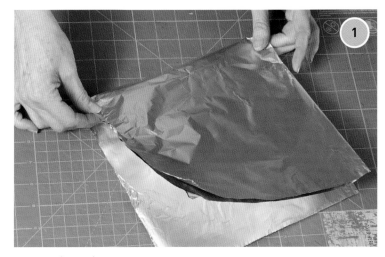

Fold an 18" (45.5 cm) -square piece of foil in half and then into quarters.

Cut an 8" (20.5 cm) square in the foil.

Remove the tracing paper to reveal the design.

INSTRUCTIONS
(for an 8" [20.5 cm] -square printing plate)

1. Cut an 18" (45.5 cm) piece of heavy-duty aluminum foil from an 18" (45.5 cm) -wide roll. Fold the foil in quarters and smooth the foil after each fold.

2. Measure, mark, and cut an 8" (20.5 cm) square in the foil.

3. Emboss the design freehand using the suggested tools or draw the design on tracing paper, tape to the foil, and draw over the tracing to transfer the design to the printing plate. Remove the tracing paper.

CREATE A FOLK ART FABRIC

Follow the steps below to create a cheery folk art–inspired fabric design. Print the background colors first by brushing diluted transparent fabric paints on the embossed aluminum. Roll undiluted transparent fabric paint over the embossed details for a second layer of printing.

Both sides of the printing plate are embossed so either side can be used. Choose one side to work with throughout so that painted and printed layers align.

INSTRUCTIONS

1. Tape the edges of the fabric to your work surface. Use the disappearing marker and ruler to mark a grid to line up the prints.

2. Use undiluted or slightly diluted transparent fabric paint directly from the bottles or mix custom colors. Use three colors (I used primary colors). Transparent fabric paint does not dry as quickly as opaque paint on the aluminum foil and tends to pick up more details on the printing plate.

3. Paint the foil printing plate using 1" (2.5 cm) foam brushes for larger color areas and small bristle brushes for details. Work quickly. It's possible that when you paint the plate for the first time, some of the paint may separate on the foil. The more the printing plate is used, the less likely this will happen.

4. Turn the printing plate over and line it up with the marked fabric grid. Roll over the unpainted side of the printing plate with a clean dense foam brayer to release the paint. The print will show the texture of the painted brushstrokes as well as some of the embossed design.

5. Use undiluted transparent fabric paint directly from the bottles or mix custom colors. (I used the same color as the painted background surrounding the flower.) Spoon about ¼ teaspoon paint onto a glass palette. Roll a dense foam brayer back and forth until it is

evenly coated with paint. Roll the paint-covered brayer across the embossed foil printing plate to cover the raised areas with paint.

6. Before printing, lightly mist the fabric to help release the painted details from the printing plate. Line up the printing plate with the painted design. Roll a clean dense foam brayer across the back side of the plate to release the paint onto the fabric. Carefully lift the printing plate off the fabric.

BRAYER RUBBINGS: Under Wraps

Printing plates made from aluminum foil, wax paper, or press-and-seal wrap, as well as freezer paper stencils, can all be slipped under the fabric for brayer rubbings (see "Three Printing Techniques" on page 30). Evenly coat a dense foam brayer with undiluted transparent or opaque paint. Roll across the fabric covering the printing plate or stencil. Shift the plate under the fabric to layer rubbings for a more elaborate design.

Slip printing plates such as this press-and-seal wrap design underneath the fabric for brayer rubbings.

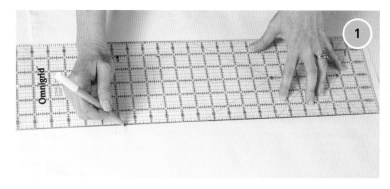

1 Tape the fabric to your padded portable work surface. Mark a grid with a disappearing marker.

2 For the first paint layer, dilute the transparent paints slightly for a more textured, painterly background.

3 Paint the embossed printing plate using 1" (2.5 cm) foam brushes for larger areas and smaller bristle brushes for details such as the center of the flower.

4 Turn the painted aluminum printing plate over, align it along the marked grid, and roll a clean dense foam brayer across the back of it.

5 To print details on top of the painted background, roll undiluted transparent fabric paint across the surface of the printing plate.

6 Lightly mist the fabric before aligning the printing plate. Roll a clean dense foam brayer across the back to release the paint.

recycled and repurposed

As I write this, my backyard trees have turned into a dazzling display of yellows, oranges, and reds. This annual transformation has me thinking about the recycled materials we use in this chapter. Boxes, catalogs, postcards, envelopes, cardboard tubes, foam containers, soda cans, and aluminum pans can all be transformed into printing blocks and stencils to create our own dazzling array of gorgeous fabrics.

In this chapter, you will curl, twist, wrap, tear, cut, incise, roll, emboss, layer, and glue recycled materials. You will create a variety of textured print blocks out of cardboard and paper. You will design bold stencils out of postcards and cereal boxes and sweet little stencils from the cellophane windows of envelopes. You will roll designs with recycled cardboard tubes, incise decorative patterns in foam containers, and cut and emboss soda cans to create ornamental printing plates.

What is so satisfying about using recycled materials is that there is always an ample supply. Many of them arrive in the mail for free or are part of the packaging for our foods. We are rescuing them from filling up landfills and putting them to good use. We are performing a bit of recycling "alchemy"— creating beautiful fabrics from trash!

The cheery, yet bold, design on the opposite page combines prints from recycled materials including a rolled paper catalog block, a layered cardboard block, and thin cardboard stencils.

This sampler of thick and thin cardboard block prints shows the range of textures and designs achievable with these very basic recycled materials.

MATERIALS

- corrugated cardboard cut into rectangles and squares (I used 3" x 4" [7.5 x 10 cm] and 4" x 4" [10 x 10 cm] sizes)
- additional corrugated cardboard (for cutting strips and designs)
- thin cardboard from boxes of cereal, pasta, food wrap, and so on
- pencil
- clear plastic gridded ruler
- self-healing cutting mat
- craft knife and/or small sharp scissors
- fine tip permanent marker
- white glue (such as Mod Podge) or gel medium
- plastic container
- foam brush
- plastic or other table covering
- masking tape
- double-sided tape
- glue stick
- wooden skewer
- shaped templates (such as plastic lids, cups, cardboard tubes, tape roll, or large cookie cutters) (optional)
- decorative hole punches and decorative edge scissors (optional)

Cardboard: The Thick and Thin of It

Look in your kitchen and you will find cardboard boxes just about everywhere. This cardboard contains our foods, cling wraps, trash bags, and more. As avid online shoppers, my husband and I frequently find heavier corrugated cardboard boxes arriving at our door. Once the packages are opened, these boxes usually make their way to the recycling bin. But instead of the bin, why not recycle them into print blocks to make beautiful fabrics for your home? Here's how!

INSTRUCTIONS

HOW TO MAKE CARDBOARD PRINT BLOCKS

Attach corrugated or thin cardboard to the corrugated cardboard blocks using the three ideas that follow. Unless otherwise noted, brush a layer of white glue or gel medium on the block before arranging the components and a second layer to secure the components and seal the blocks after the first layer dries.

Arrange strips and shapes of cardboard or score corrugated cardboard blocks for a wide range of print block possibilities.

1. Cardboard Strips

Cut ¼" (6 mm) strips of corrugated card-board or ¼" to ½" (6 mm to 1.3 cm) strips of thin cardboard. Create designs in the following ways:

- Arrange strips with the flat side facing up.
- Arrange strips on edge (especially effective with corrugated strips).
- Roll strips around a wooden skewer to make tight spirals. Use tape to keep them from unrolling.
- Roll strips and leave them untaped so that the spirals unwind slightly.
- Weave strips of thin cardboard. Cut parallel or alternating slits in a flat piece of thin cardboard that are wide enough to slip the strips through to simulate weaving. Cover a corrugated cardboard block with double-sided tape and press the woven piece onto the block.

2. Layered Cardboard Shapes

- Cut shapes out of thin or corrugated cardboard. Use a permanent marker to draw freehand or trace around templates. Cut the shapes out with a craft knife or sharp scissors.
- Punch out thin cardboard shapes with decorative hole punches or cut shapes with decorative edge scissors.
- Glue shapes to each other with a glue stick and arrange on the cardboard block.

3. Cut and Peel Designs

Draw bold designs on a corrugated cardboard block using templates or a ruler. Score the cardboard with a craft knife and carefully remove the thin paper layer from some areas of the design to expose the corrugated texture. (See above.)

TIP: Cardboard Combinations

Create blocks that combine corrugated textures with thin cardboard shapes. Peel away the paper to expose the corrugated layer. Cut motifs, such as a leaf, from thin cardboard to glue on top. Add details with smaller pieces of thin cardboard, such as the veins of the leaf. Prints with these blocks combine texture with layered designs for visually interesting fabrics. (See the leaf designs on the fabric on page 76.)

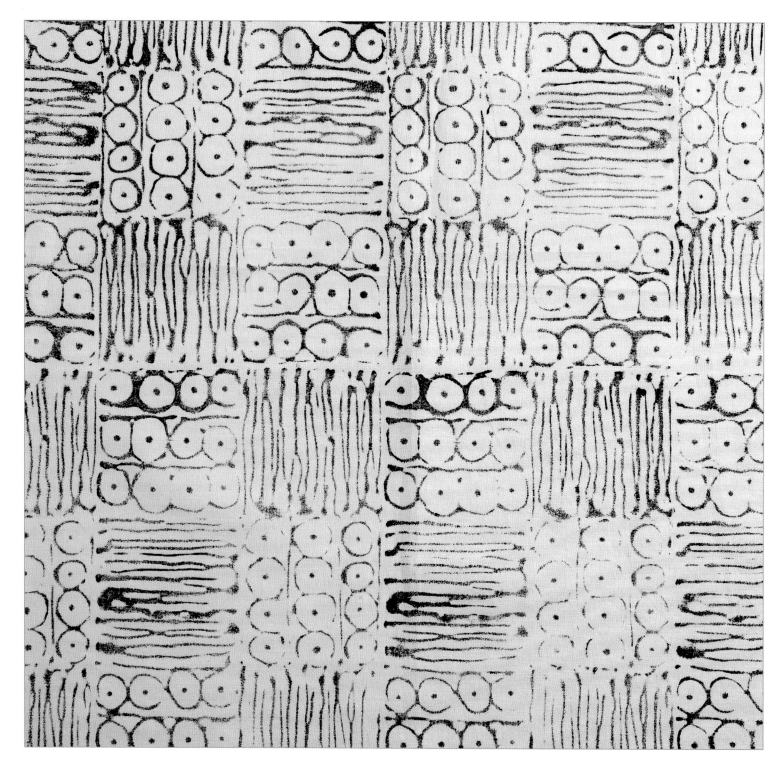

Uneven, organic lines are characteristic of prints made with hot glue blocks.

MATERIALS

- corrugated cardboard cut into rectangular or square blocks sealed with a layer of white glue or gel medium
- hot glue gun
- hot glue sticks
- pencil
- piece of aluminum foil

HOW TO MAKE HOT GLUE BLOCKS

The slightly uneven organic lines you can print with hot glue blocks are like no other. The blocks are also quick to make. The "glue" (really thermoplastic adhesive) comes in cylindrical sticks that fit into the back of an electric "gun" that heats up and melts the stick. The melted adhesive flows through the gun's tip and is controlled by pumping a trigger. The glue cools and hardens in just a couple of minutes. (Caution: Melted hot glue can cause burns. Be very careful not to touch the glue before it cools. Also, do not touch the tip of the glue gun. An alternative to hot glue is tacky glue. Tacky glue designs can take up to a day to dry so plan ahead.)

INSTRUCTIONS

1. Draw simple designs or patterns with a pencil on the corrugated cardboard.

2. Heat up the glue following the manufacturer's instructions. Place the glue gun on the foil to catch any excess drips. Squeeze the trigger to release the glue. (Add new glue sticks as needed. Pump the trigger at regular intervals so the glue releases more easily and evenly.)

Draw simple pencil designs on the cardboard block.

Squeeze the trigger to release hot glue onto the block.

CARDBOARD STENCILS

In chapter 4, you learned how to design stencils using freezer paper. Because freezer paper is translucent, it's easy to slip your design under the paper to trace. But what if you want to design a stencil using opaque materials, such as recycled cereal boxes and postcards? Below are some approaches to creating cardboard stencils.

Direct Drawing on Cardboard

Use a permanent marker to draw a design directly on thin cardboard. For simple, shaped stencils, trace around shaped templates and add details. Cut out the design using a craft knife. (See A.)

Draw or Photocopy a Design

Draw a stencil design on a separate sheet of white computer printer paper or photocopy a design from source material. Glue the paper design to the cardboard and cut it out with a craft knife. (See B.)

Folded Paper Design

Cut a piece of white paper the size and shape of your final stencil. Use a template for a circular design. Fold the paper in quarters or eighths or make diagonal folds. Use a craft knife or small sharp scissors to cut out shapes. Glue the cut paper design to a piece of black construction paper to see how the final stencil design will appear when it is printed. With this technique, the bridges (see page 64) are already built into the design. Photocopy the design and glue it to the cardboard. Cut out the black areas of the design using a craft knife. (See C.)

If you don't have access to a photocopy machine, trace your design onto tracing paper with a graphite pencil. Flip the tracing over onto the cardboard and retrace to transfer the design. (See D.)

MATERIALS

- thin cardboard, including cereal or other similar weight boxes, postcards, or card stock–weight cardboard
- white computer printer paper
- black construction paper
- tracing paper
- craft knife
- small, sharp scissors (optional)
- glue stick
- shaped templates: plastic lids, cups, cardboard tubes, tape roll, large cookie cutters
- pencil
- permanent marker
- photocopy machine or computer printer

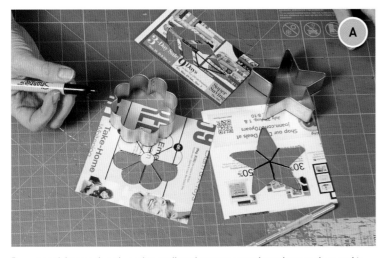

Draw stencil designs directly on thin cardboard or trace around templates such as cookie cutters. Add bridges before cutting out your designs.

Draw stencil designs on white paper or photocopy a design. Glue the design onto thin cardboard and cut out with a craft knife.

Photocopy a cut paper design, glue the copy to thin cardboard, and cut out the black sections.

Trace a design with graphite pencil and transfer it to thin cardboard before cutting.

Turn catalog pages into an endless variety of print blocks: Roll tubes, twist strips into spirals, or glue and cut page sections to create designs.

Junk Mail Jackpot

When I hear the metallic thunk of the mailbox shutting, I know it's time to see the day's delivery of recyclable goodies. As the saying goes, "One man's trash is another man's treasure." These days I welcome the catalogs, bills, and postcard advertisements. I feel like the lucky jackpot winner, plotting how I will transform my "winnings" into print blocks and stencils. I get goose bumps thinking about all the gorgeous fabrics I'll design from these free materials that get delivered right to my door!

DECONSTRUCTING CLOTHING CATALOGS

Below are ideas for turning those ubiquitous clothing catalogs into print blocks. Feel free to substitute other paper recyclables, including magazines, newspapers, and even paper bags!

INSTRUCTIONS

Create paper components to attach to corrugated cardboard blocks. Unless otherwise noted, brush a layer of white glue or gel medium on the block before arranging the components and a second layer to secure the components and seal the blocks after the first layer dries.

- Cut ¼" (6 mm) strips of paper and tear into small pieces. Randomly arrange the paper bits onto the wet glue or gel medium.
- Cut 1" (2.5 cm) strips by the width of a catalog page. Wrap strips around a wooden skewer to make tight paper tubes. Tape along the edge to keep them from unrolling.

- Cut a 6" x 8" (16 x 20.5 cm) piece from a catalog page. Roll from the short side. Make either a very tight roll (¼" [6 mm] diameter) or a looser roll (½" [1.3 cm] diameter). Tape along the edge to keep it from unrolling. Cut ½" [1.3 cm] cross-section pieces with a craft knife.

POSTCARD PIZZAZZ

Recycle postcard advertisements by turning them into detailed hand-cut stencils (see "Cardboard Stencils" on page 82). Use decorative hole punches to make easy, playful stencils and glue the punched pieces to corrugated cardboard for jazzy block designs. (See "Cardboard: The Thick and Thin of It" on page 78 for more ideas.)

This fabric created with thin cardboard stencils has lots of movement and "pop" because of its bright colors and repetition of circular shapes.

Recycled paper blocks can be used for both background texture and focal blocks as seen in this fabric.

MATERIALS

- envelopes with cellophane windows
- craft knife or small sharp scissors
- self-healing cutting mat
- fine tip permanent marker
- small decorative hole punches
- masking tape

A combination of three simple cellophane stencils turn into a printed cluster of blooming cherry trees.

Crumple Paper

Manipulate a catalog page until it softens and then:

- Arrange the softened paper over a cardboard block so it has interesting folds and creases. Tape the excess to the back of the block.
- Flatten out the crumpled page and cut 1" (2.5 cm) -strips the length of the page. Twist the strips and then roll them into tight spirals. Tape to hold in place.

Glue Pages Together

Brush white glue or gel medium on each page of a ten-page section to glue them together. After they're dry, cut the glued pages into ¼" (6 mm) strips. Fold the strips or roll them into spirals. Tape the components as needed.

SIMPLE AND SWEET: CELLOPHANE WINDOW STENCILS

Here's a reason to be happy when those bills arrive in the mail! Most of them come in envelopes with cellophane windows that can be turned into sweet little stencils. Combine prints of these miniature stencils to add a whimsical touch to small home décor projects or children's clothing.

INSTRUCTIONS

1. Cut away the back of the envelope. Trim down the front side with the cellophane window, leaving about ½" (1.3 cm) of paper around the window.

2. Draw simple designs on the cellophane with the permanent marker.

3. Tape the envelope to your cutting mat. Cut out the designs. Be careful not to tear the delicate cellophane while you're cutting. Or use small decorative hole punches for quick and easy stencil designs. Try punches with flowers, hearts, or stars.

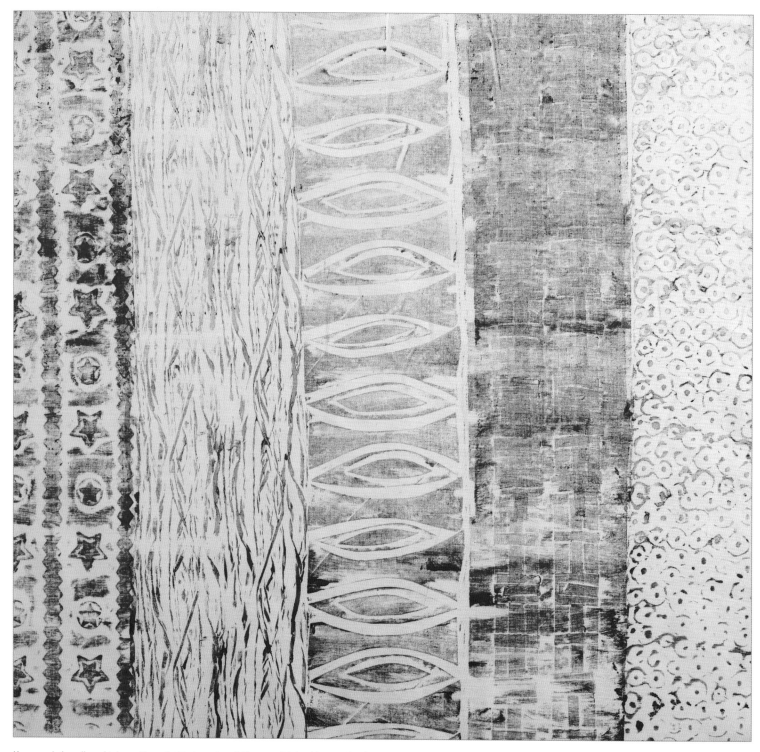

Use recycled cardboard tubes with applied textures to quickly cover fabric with repeating designs.

- assorted cardboard tubes in different sizes and degrees of sturdiness (I recommend sturdy tubes, such as those that hold plastic wrap, which fit perfectly over dense foam brayers)
- rubber bands
- string or twine
- masking tape
- craft knife or scissors
- clear plastic gridded ruler
- self-healing cutting mat
- measuring tape
- #2 pencil or pen
- 4" (10 cm) dense foam brayers
- white glue (such as Mod Podge) or gel medium
- plastic container
- foam brush
- plastic or other table covering
- recycled postcards, cereal boxes, or other thin cardboard
- recycled paper
- double-sided tape
- glue stick
- hot glue gun with extra hot glue sticks
- decorative hole punches and decorative edge scissors (optional)

On a Roll: Fabric Designs from Cardboard Tubes

Rolled designs using recycled cardboard tubes are an effective way to quickly apply a repeating design or texture on your fabric. Because the circumference of most tubes is small, designs will be darker at the start and begin to fade the farther the tube is rolled. Use this as part of your planned fabric or add more paint to the tube and match up the design at the point where it starts to fade. Rolled textures add richness to fabrics and can serve as backgrounds for your recycled print blocks and stencils.

PREPARING THE CARDBOARD TUBES

Any type of cardboard tube can be used for a rolled design. Here are ways to prepare them for printing.

- Create tubes to slip over 4" (10 cm) dense foam brayers. Choose sturdy cardboard tubes with an interior diameter large enough to fit over the foam brayers. Measure and cut 3.75" (9.5 cm) lengths from each cardboard tube.
- Create rolled fabric designs with intact sturdy cardboard tubes that are 12" (30.5 cm) or longer. Mark an area in the center of the tube for your design, leaving at least 3" (7.5 cm) on each end as a handle for rolling across the fabric.
- Your cardboard tube designs will last longer if they are sealed with a thin coat of white glue or gel medium. Seal the tubes before applying hot glue designs or wrapping with rubber bands. For other designs using cardboard, string, or paper, seal the tubes after applying the materials.

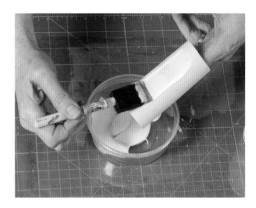

Seal cardboard tubes with white glue or gel medium to make them more durable.

A LIST OF "TUBULAR" DESIGN IDEAS

- Wrap rubber bands around a cardboard tube.
- Cover the cardboard tube with double-sided tape and then wrap with string or twine.
- Scrunch recycled paper until it softens and then roll and twist it around a cardboard tube covered with double-sided tape.
- Cut and layer designs from recycled postcards or cereal boxes and glue them to a cardboard tube. Use decorative edge scissors to cut cardboard strips.
- Create designs with decorative hole punches. Punch designs directly into a thin cardboard tube or punch designs from other thin recycled cardboard to layer and glue on a tube.
- Use a craft knife or small sharp scissors to cut slits or other designs in a thin cardboard tube.
- Tear or cut strips of masking tape and layer on a cardboard tube.
- Carefully apply hot glue to a cardboard tube. Create simple designs such as lines, dots, circles, and so on.

Use "tools" such as a small fork or key to incise designs in recycled foam. Make the focal block stand out from the background by first printing with an unmarked foam shape in a contrasting color, as shown here.

MATERIALS

- thin foam containers, plates, and/or meat trays, thoroughly cleaned of food residue prior to use
- craft knife or scissors
- clear plastic gridded ruler
- self-healing cutting mat
- assorted "tools" to create designs in the foam (such as eating utensils, pens, keys, screws, and so on)
- masking tape
- cups or containers that can be used as templates to trace shapes onto the foam (optional)
- corrugated cardboard cut into shapes to back foam (optional)
- double-sided tape for mounting foam onto cardboard (see "Helpful Hint" on page 91)

Making Your Mark: Designing Print Blocks from Recycled Foam

I admit that the young explorer came out in me while working with recycled foam containers and trays. I was excited to discover a little catchall box in one of my kitchen drawers. Inside was a treasure trove of mark-making "tools": keys, screws, staples, paper clips, coins, nails, picture hangers, safety pins, and brass paper fasteners. Each item offered up new possibilities, and I became totally absorbed in how many different types of marks I could make in the foam. Soon I was combining marks, spontaneously creating patterns and designs. Enjoy making your own unique marks in recycled foam and print one-of-a-kind fabrics!

INSTRUCTIONS

1. Cut the clean foam containers, plates, or trays into different shapes such as squares, circles, narrow strips, and organic shapes. To make shaped blocks, trace around templates.

2. Test out different mark-making tools on pieces of foam. Keep an open mind about the kinds of marks you can make with each tool. Some tools can make more than one type of mark. For example, a fork can make stipple markings with the tips of the prongs, parallel straight or wavy lines by pulling the prongs across the foam, and even concentric circles.

3. After testing out your tools, combine different marks to create a series of interesting print blocks. Save some unmarked foam to print with focal blocks. (See fabric above.)

1

Cut out flat sections from recycled foam containers and make into shapes.

2

Use "tools" such as this small fork to incise designs in the foam.

3

A selection of foam blocks showing a variety of incised designs.

HELPFUL HINT:
How to "Handle" Foam Print Blocks

Removing flat foam blocks from fabric during printing can be tricky. Here are two ideas to make it easier:

1. Create a masking tape handle. Attach a folded strip of masking tape to the back of the foam. Grasp the handle to remove the foam print block after printing.

2. Mount your foam onto corrugated cardboard. Cut the cardboard to the shape of the foam and attach with strips of double-sided tape. The additional thickness of the corrugated cardboard is easier to remove from the fabric.

A simple handle made from a folded strip of masking tape makes it easier to print with recycled foam blocks.

MATERIALS

- clean aluminum soda cans and baking pans
- cutting tools (such as craft knife, scissors, or tin snips)
- embossing tools (such as ballpoint pen, wooden end of a paint brush)
- permanent marker
- protective gloves (optional)

This fabric combines prints made with a cut and embossed soda can (butterfly motif) and a stencil created by cutting rectangular openings in an aluminum cake pan.

Artful Aluminum: Create Decorative Shapes from Recycled Cans and Pans

Turn recycled aluminum soda cans and baking pans into shaped print blocks. Cut out decorative motifs such as hearts and stars or simple animal shapes. Emboss these designs to add texture and character. Get inspired by the shapes of Mexican tin art ornaments! Print multiple layers of color to add depth to your fabric designs.

INSTRUCTIONS

1. Cut off the top and bottom of the soda can. Slice the remaining cylinder so you can work on a flat piece. Cut off the sides of the baking pan so you can easily work with the flat bottom.

2. Work with simple shapes. Draw directly on the aluminum with the permanent marker or trace around templates such as cookie cutters or found objects. Fold the soda can aluminum in half to create symmetrical designs such as a heart or butterfly. Most aluminum pans already have embossed designs. You can play off of these to create motifs. The cake pan I used had a large embossed eight-pointed star that I was able to turn into a bold sun design. (See fabric on page 6.)

3. Cut out your shapes. For the simplest shapes you can use scissors. More complicated designs will require a craft knife.

TIP: Accentuating Embossed Designs

For more defined decorative details try this: Draw into the aluminum with a ballpoint pen and then flip it over to see the raised design. Accentuate the embossed lines by drawing "valleys" on either side.

4. Emboss decorative designs in the aluminum shapes. A ballpoint pen works best with the tougher soda can aluminum. Use the wooden end of a paintbrush to flatten out unwanted logo designs in the softer aluminum pan. See the tip on accentuating embossed designs.

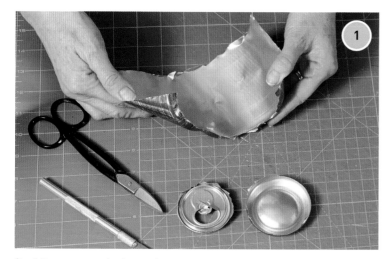

Carefully cut apart an aluminum soda can.

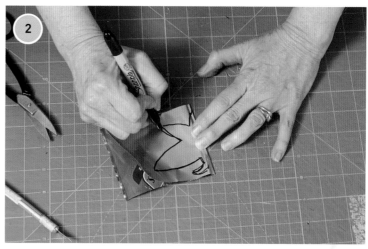

Draw a simple design, such as a butterfly, along the fold with a permanent marker.

Use small sharp scissors to cut out the shape.

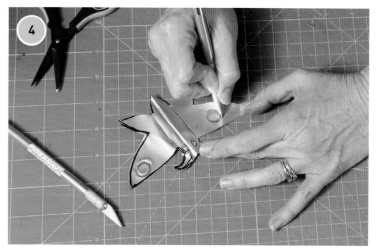

Emboss designs with a ballpoint pen.

- Basic Tool Kit (see page 13)
- stencils, print blocks, plates, or textured tubes
- 20" x 30" (51 x 76 cm) piece of ½" (1.3 cm) -thick upholstery foam
- 22" x 32" (56 x 81.5 cm) piece of muslin or cotton fabric
- additional dense foam brayers
- additional sturdy cardboard tubes

Here's an example of direct printing with a recycled cardboard block.

Printing with Recycled Materials

After you create stencils, print blocks, printing plates, and textured tubes using recycled materials, it's time to print with them.

INSTRUCTIONS

1. Tape the edges of the fabric to your work surface.

2. Mix up colors of opaque fabric paint or use colors directly from the bottles. If you are printing with embossed aluminum shapes, you can opt to use undiluted transparent fabric paint instead. When mixing a custom color, start with the lightest color and gradually add darker colors.

DIRECT PRINTING

For direct printing with cardboard blocks, paper blocks, incised foam, and embossed aluminum, do the following:

1. Spoon ¼ teaspoon paint onto a glass palette. Roll a dense foam brayer back and forth until it is evenly coated with paint.

2. Use the paint-covered brayer to roll an even coat of paint on the print block.

3. Turn the block over onto the fabric and press down to release the paint onto the fabric. Use the extra padding covered with muslin to print with more dimensional blocks. Optional: Roll a clean dense foam brayer over the back of an embossed aluminum shape to release the paint.

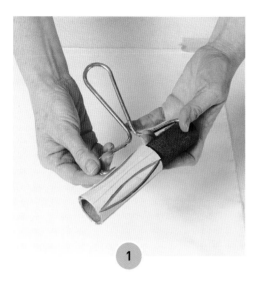

1

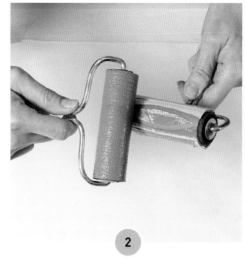

2

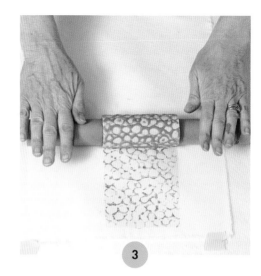

3

Slip a sturdy cardboard tube with designs onto a clean dense foam brayer.

Apply paint to the cardboard tube design by rolling a paint-covered brayer up and down the design.

To print tube designs with larger diameters, slip a sturdy tube inside and roll.

PRINTING WITH CARDBOARD TUBES

1. Pull one of the metal ends out of a clean dense foam brayer and slip on a 3.75" (9.5 cm) sturdy cardboard tube with designs.

2. To roll an even coat of paint onto the cardboard tube design, hold the brayer with the cardboard tube perpendicular to the paint-covered brayer. Roll the paint-covered brayer up and down the cardboard tube design. The brayer with the cardboard tube will spin. Continue applying paint until the design is completely covered. For tubes with larger diameters than the brayer or sturdy tubes with centered designs, use this same technique but manually turn the tubes as you apply the paint.

3. Roll the tube-covered brayer or sturdy cardboard tube with designs across the fabric to release the paint. To print using a cardboard tube with a larger diameter than the brayer, slip a sturdy tube with a smaller diameter inside the cardboard tube with the design. Place your hands on the ends of the sturdy tube and roll.

STENCILING

To apply paint to cardboard or aluminum stencils do the following:

1. Tape the stencil to the fabric.

2. Pick up paint with a foam dauber. Press it on the glass a few times to release excess paint.

3. Daub the paint across the stencil design.

BRAYER RUBBINGS

Slip flat print blocks, printing plates, or stencils under your fabric. Use a paint-covered dense foam brayer to roll paint over the fabric covering the print block or stencil to pick up the design.

irresistible:
FABRIC RESISTS USING KITCHEN INGREDIENTS

A resist is any material applied to fabric that prevents dye or paint from reaching the fabric's surface. Masks and stencils are types of resists in which parts of the fabric are covered while others are exposed to paint. Other resists include pastes, syrups, and gels that need to first dry on the fabric to form a paint barrier. We'll explore these in this chapter.

Most of the resist recipes in this chapter are the result of many months of experimentation with kitchen materials. In addition, I had to devise ways to prevent paint from seeping under resists and find the best ways to apply the resists to fabric. What I found and continue to find so fascinating about working with resists is that each one has a unique mark or texture. For example, cooked confectioners' sugar syrup creates a rich velvety texture, while uncooked wheat flour paste has its own characteristic cracked lines reminiscent of wax batik. These unique surface textures can be taken into account and used to full advantage when designing fabrics.

This chapter will introduce you to resist recipes and application techniques. Each technique has a list of suggested resists to use. Get comfortable working with the suggested combinations of resist and application technique, and then have fun layering resist textures. Once you get started you can't help but see the tremendous potential for using resists to add texture and pattern to fabric.

A paste of wheat flour and water was spread across the painted background on the image opposite and "scratched" away using a fork and found objects.

MATERIALS

- 1 cup (125 g) all-purpose white wheat flour
- 1 cup (235 ml) cold water
- large bowl (such as a 1¾-quart [1.7 L] Pyrex bowl)
- liquid and dry measuring cups
- wire whisk

Uncooked wheat flour paste is easy to make and can be applied in many ways. Create designs like you see here by slipping hot glue print blocks under the fabric for rubbings with a plastic spreader.

Resist Recipes

The quantities of listed ingredients will make enough resist to cover at least one fat quarter of fabric. It's best to use the resists as soon as you make them, especially the gelatin resists, which gel within a short period of time. Liquid dishwashing soap is the exception because it can be used directly from the bottle at any time.

UNCOOKED WHEAT FLOUR PASTE RESIST

This simple mixture of white wheat flour and water is the best resist recipe to use to simulate the characteristic crackle designs of wax batik. Scratch designs or words into a thin layer of paste or try a rubbing using a plastic spreader. (See "Resist Application Technique" on page 105 for other application techniques using this versatile resist.)

INSTRUCTIONS

1. Pour the cold water into the bowl.

2. Gradually add the flour to the water while stirring with a wire whisk.

3. Continue stirring the mixture until it is a smooth paste the consistency of pancake batter. Add more flour or water as needed to reach that consistency.

MATERIALS

- 3 tablespoons (41 g) baking powder
- 1½ cups (352 ml) water
- 3-quart (3 L) cooking pot
- liquid measuring cup
- tablespoon
- wire whisk
- trivet
- stove or hot plate

Spreading and cracking dried resist and printing using a spreader are two techniques that work well with cooked baking powder resist.

COOKED BAKING POWDER RESIST

Cooked baking powder is great fun to concoct with its bubbling "special effects"! It has a very distinctive crackle, with small cracks that tend to run parallel to each other. This resist works best on cotton fabric and has a tendency to flake off silk as it dries.

INSTRUCTIONS

1. Pour the water into the pot. Add the baking powder and stir with the wire whisk. As the baking powder dissolves it releases bicarbonate of soda, causing the mixture to fizz.

2. Once the mixture stops fizzing, turn the stove to medium heat and continue to stir the mixture. It will start to slowly bubble in about two minutes and turn into foam the consistency of whipped egg whites. If the foam starts to rise up too high in the pot, turn down the heat.

3. Continue cooking and stirring the mixture for two more minutes. Remove the cooked baking powder resist from the stove and set the pot on a trivet to cool. The resist will have the consistency of a thick milky liquid. You can use the resist once it is cool enough to handle safely.

GELATIN RESIST

After much experimentation with different ratios and temperatures of water mixed in with the gelatin powder, I worked out the two recipes that follow. Gelatin gels quickly, making these recipes time-sensitive. Specific application techniques work best with each recipe. Recipe #1 will start to thicken almost immediately after stirring in the water. Spread it across your fabric or apply with a bristle brush before it completely gels and becomes too difficult to work with. Recipe #2 has more water and gels a bit more slowly. Some techniques, such as dribbling from a spoon or nature printing, need to be performed first while the gelatin is still liquid. Try other techniques, such as stenciling or printing with a plastic spreader, after the resist starts to gel.

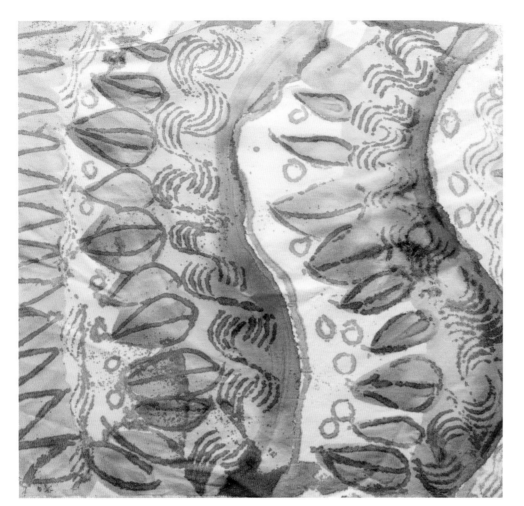

MATERIALS

- 4 packets unflavored powdered gelatin (total net weight 1 ounce [28 g])
- 1 cup (235 ml) cold water
- large bowl
- liquid measuring cup
- wire whisk

Scratch designs in a layer of gelatin applied to fabric with a plastic spreader. After painting and removing the resist, notice the granular spotted textures characteristic of gelatin resist.

Recipe #1

A distinguishing characteristic of this recipe is the granular spotting that occurs after painting over the resist, adding texture to fabric designs.

INSTRUCTIONS

1. Pour the unflavored powdered gelatin into the bowl.

2. Pour the water into the bowl and use a wire whisk to stir the mixture until it is thoroughly dissolved.

3. Use the resist just as it starts to thicken.

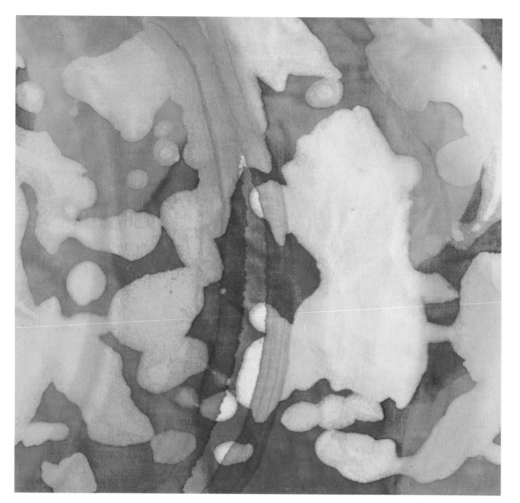

- 4 packets of unflavored powdered gelatin (total net weight 1 ounce [28 g])
- 1 cup (235 ml) cold water
- ½ cup (118 ml) boiling or very hot water
- large bowl
- liquid measuring cup
- wire whisk

Dribble this gelatin recipe from a spoon to achieve designs with fine granular shading.

Recipe #2

After painting, notice the fine granular shading around the edges left by this resist. This effect is most apparent when the resist is used in its liquid state for spoon dribbles or printing with leaves.

INSTRUCTIONS

1. Pour the unflavored powdered gelatin into the bowl.

2. Pour the cold water into the bowl and whisk the mixture until it is thoroughly dissolved.

3. Add the boiling or very hot water and stir with the wire whisk.

MATERIALS

- 1 cup (120 g) confectioners' sugar
- ½ cup (118 ml) water
- large microwave-safe bowl (such as a 1¾-quart [1.7 L] Pyrex bowl)
- liquid and dry measuring cups
- wire whisk
- oven mitts
- trivet
- plastic wrap
- microwave oven

Brush the confectioners' sugar resist on the fabric and allow it to dry before applying paint. Apply a second layer of resist with monoprinting. This resist leaves soft, velvety marks on the fabric.

COOKED CONFECTIONERS' SUGAR RESIST

When combined, microwaved confectioners' sugar and water become a light syrup that makes a beautiful resist. The marks created using cooked confectioners' sugar have a soft, velvety appearance.

INSTRUCTIONS

1. Pour the water into a microwave-safe bowl.

2. Add the confectioners' sugar and whisk to dissolve.

3. Cover the bowl with plastic wrap and cook the mixture for five minutes on high heat in a microwave oven.

4. Using oven mitts, remove the bowl of bubbling, hot syrup from the microwave. Be very careful when removing the plastic wrap. Let the syrup cool enough to be handled safely. To make a smaller or larger amount of this resist, adjust the microwave cooking time. The cooked mixture should be the consistency of light syrup.

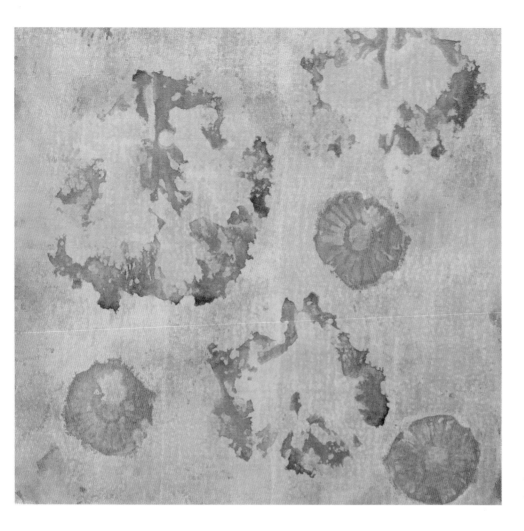

Use liquid dishwashing soap for brayer rubbings with flat textures. Brush soap on leaves and apply to a carved turnip with a plastic spreader before direct printing.

LIQUID DISHWASHING SOAP RESIST

What could be better than a fabric resist used straight from the bottle that dries quickly on fabric and washes out with ease? Liquid dishwashing soap is a great go-to resist for all those reasons and more. Try drawing designs with a plastic squeeze bottle, monoprinting on glass, or making brayer rubbings on fabric. Designs created with this resist will have crisper edges compared with the soft edges left by the confectioners' sugar resist.

Roll wet resists, such as liquid dishwashing soap, across a carved block or flat texture and create printed images that resist paint. The resulting designs will appear as the negative to those printed with fabric paint. (See B on page 109.)

Use a plastic spreader to spread a thin, even layer of resist across the fabric.

Resist Application Techniques

Now it's time to see the various surface design effects possible using the simple kitchen ingredients we've stirred and cooked into resists. Each technique that follows includes the materials needed and the steps for successfully applying a resist to the fabric. In addition, there is a list of suggested resists for each application technique.

PREPARING TO APPLY RESISTS TO FABRIC

Before getting started, here are some preparation tips and recommended tools. The thicker resists, such as uncooked wheat flour paste, cooked baking powder, and gelatin recipe #1, will need extra help penetrating the fabric's fibers. Mist the fabric with water before applying these resists. Rubbing with a plastic spreader is one exception to this rule. Starting with wet or dry fabric for this technique does not significantly alter the end result. The "wetter" resists, such as gelatin recipe #2, cooked confectioners' sugar, and liquid dishwashing soap should be applied to dry fabric.

Tools

Many of the tools needed to apply resists will be familiar because we used them in earlier chapters. In addition, carved erasers or print blocks (see "Carving Large" on page 106) and found objects, such as pill bottles and bottle caps, will come in handy for some of the techniques below. Additional tools needed include:

1. Plastic spreader. Buy this at an auto supply shop. Plastic spreaders usually come packaged in a set of three different sizes and are used for auto body repairs. I generally like to use the smallest size because it's easy to handle when applying a resist to a print block. Feel free to substitute a small squeegee or old plastic credit card.

2. Plastic squeeze bottles. Have different sizes of these bottles with different size tips available. Thicker resists will require larger squeeze bottles with bigger holed tips. Recycled condiment or liquid dishwashing soap bottles work well. Syrup and liquid resists flow nicely through fine tips. I use special small plastic detail writers purchased from art supply stores.

3. Small plastic funnel. This is a helpful aid for getting the resists into the plastic squeeze bottles. Have a number of sizes available for use.

DIRECT APPLICATION TECHNIQUES

Use tools to apply resists directly to the fabric's surface. Each tool in combination with each suggested resist makes distinct textural marks on the fabric. Tape the fabric to a padded portable work surface and mist if needed before applying the resist (see "Preparing to Apply Resists to Fabric" on page 105).

- **Spread and crackle.** Pour or spoon the resist onto the fabric and use a plastic spreader to spread a thin layer across the fabric's surface. Let the resist dry completely before manipulating it to form small cracks. Suggested resists: uncooked wheat flour paste, cooked baking powder, cooked confectioners' sugar. (See A.)

- **Spread and scratch.** Pour or spoon the resist onto the fabric. Use a plastic spreader to spread a thin layer of resist across the fabric's surface. Let the resist set for a few minutes before scratching designs or words with "tools" such as a wooden skewer, plastic fork, or found objects. Suggested resists: uncooked wheat flour paste, cooked baking powder, gelatin recipe #1. (See B.)

- **Dribbling.** Dribble resist from a spoon to create free-form designs. Suggested resists: uncooked wheat flour paste, gelatin recipe #2 (before it gels), cooked confectioners' sugar, liquid dishwashing soap. (See C.)

- **Draw with a plastic squeeze bottle.** Choose plastic bottles with holes of varying sizes to accommodate different resists. Draw shapes or designs or write words with resists using this technique. Suggested resists: uncooked wheat flour paste, cooked confectioners' sugar, liquid dishwashing soap. (See D.)

- **Apply with a brush.** Different sizes and types of brushes make different marks on the fabric. Each listed resist will bring additional unique characteristics to these marks. Suggested resists: uncooked wheat flour paste, cooked baking powder, gelatin recipe #1, gelatin recipe #2 (before it gels), cooked confectioners' sugar, liquid dishwashing soap. (See E.)

CARVING LARGE

To print with resists, you'll need large novelty erasers or soft, easy-to-carve print blocks such as Speedball Speedy Carve. Use linoleum cutters to carve designs directly into the block or trace a design and transfer it before carving.

Carve designs in large novelty erasers or easy-to-carve print blocks to use when printing with resists.

After the resist has completely dried on the fabric, remove it from your work surface, and manipulate it to form small cracks.

Use "tools" such as a plastic fork, wooden skewer, or bottle cap to remove resist from the fabric.

Create free-form designs on fabric by dribbling resists from a spoon.

Choose plastic squeeze bottles with holes appropriate for your chosen resist to draw designs or write words directly on the fabric.

Use different sizes and types of brushes to make unique marks with resists on your fabric.

PRINTING WITH RESISTS

Print with resists using the following techniques. Tape the fabric to a padded portable work surface and mist if needed before applying the resist (see "Preparing to Apply Resists to Fabric" on page 105).

- **Print with a plastic spreader.** Spoon or squeeze resist onto a carved print block. Use the spreader to push the resist into the cut-away areas of the block and remove any excess from the surface. Turn the block over onto the fabric and press to release the resist. Suggested resists: uncooked wheat flour paste, cooked baking powder, gelatin recipe #2 (after it starts to gel), cooked confectioners' sugar, liquid dishwashing soap. (See A.)

- **Print with a dense foam brayer.** Spoon or squeeze resist onto a glass palette. Roll a dense foam brayer back and forth across the glass until it is evenly coated with the resist and then roll the resist over the block design. Turn the block over onto the fabric and press to release the resist. Suggested resists: cooked confectioners' sugar, liquid dishwashing soap. (See B.)

- **Print with leaves.** Place a lettuce or herb leaf on a glass palette and brush resist onto the more textured side. Turn the leaf over onto the fabric, cover it with a paper towel, and press to release the resist. Remove the paper towel but leave the leaf in place. Brush the resist across the edges of the leaf to better define the image. Suggested resists: gelatin recipe #2 (before it gels), cooked confectioners' sugar, liquid dishwashing soap. (See C.)

- **Monoprint on glass.** Draw designs on a glass palette using squeeze bottles filled with resist. Turn the glass palette over onto the fabric and press to release the resist. The design will spread a bit on the fabric. Suggested resists: cooked confectioners' sugar, liquid dishwashing soap. (See D.)

STENCILS AND MASKS

Create your own cardboard stencil designs or use commercial stencils with this technique. Use a plastic spreader to apply the thicker resists and a brush to apply the liquid resists. If you plan to repeat designs, wipe off the stencils between printings. Tape the fabric to a padded portable work surface and mist it if needed before applying the resist. (See "Preparing to Apply Resists to Fabric" on page 105.)

- **Stencil resists with a plastic spreader.** Prepare the stencil by taping 2" (5 cm) masking tape on one edge. Tape the stencil onto the fabric. Spoon resist onto the tape flap, which acts as a holding area making it easier to evenly apply across the openings in the stencil. Use a plastic spreader to pull the resist across the stencil. The resist will fill the cut-away areas of the stencil. Suggested resists: uncooked wheat flour paste, cooked baking powder, gelatin recipe #2 (after it gels). (See E.)

- **Stencil resists with a foam brush.** Tape the stencil onto the fabric. Pour or squeeze some resist into a plastic container. Dip the brush in the container and brush it across the side to remove any excess resist. Carefully brush the resist across the openings in the stencil design. Suggested resists: gelatin recipe #2 (before it gels), cooked confectioners' sugar, liquid dishwashing soap.

TIP: Resists on Flat Kitchen Textures

Try rolling resist onto flat kitchen textures such as shelf liner or gripper pads (see chapter 2). Turn the resist-covered texture over onto the fabric and press to release the resist.

Use a plastic spreader to apply resist to a carved block.

Roll an even layer of resist onto a carved block.

Remove the paper towel but keep the leaf on the fabric. Treat the leaf like a stencil and brush resist across the edges.

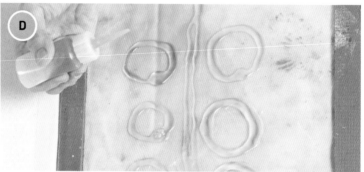

Use a plastic squeeze bottle filled with resist to draw designs on a piece of glass.

Pull the resist across the stencil with the plastic spreader.

Brush the resist across the openings in the freezer paper mask.

Slip a flat texture block, such as hot glue on a cardboard block, under the fabric.

FREEZER PAPER MASKS

When working with thicker resists, simple, bold designs cut in a sheet of freezer paper or torn strips work best. Iron the mask to the fabric. Tape the fabric with attached mask to a padded portable work surface and lightly mist it (avoid getting the paper too wet) if needed before applying the resist. (See "Preparing to Apply Resists to Fabric" on page 105.)

- **Use a plastic spreader to apply the resist.**
  Spoon some resist onto the fabric and use the plastic spreader to pull it across the freezer paper mask designs. Suggested resists: uncooked wheat flour paste, cooked baking powder, gelatin recipe #2 (after it gels).

- **Use a foam brush to apply the resist.**
  Pour or squeeze some resist into a container. Dip the brush in the container and brush it across the side to remove any excess resist. Carefully brush the resist across the openings or around the edges of the freezer paper mask designs. Suggested resists: gelatin recipe #2 (before it gels), cooked confectioners' sugar, liquid dishwashing soap. (See A.)

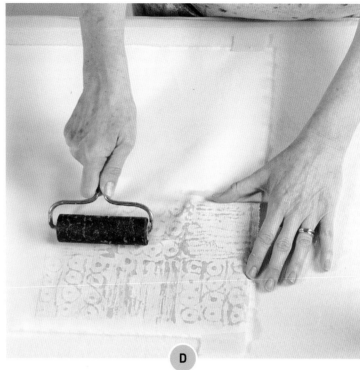

Spoon the resist onto the fabric and pull it across the area covering the texture block.

Roll a resist-covered brayer over the fabric covering the texture block.

RUBBINGS

Rubbings made with either a spreader or brayer create beautiful background textures and patterns that can stand on their own or can be enhanced with additional printing or stenciling. Tape the fabric to a padded portable work surface. You do not need to mist the fabric before applying the resists. Position a flat texture or carved block or textured material under the fabric. (See B.)

- **Use a plastic spreader to apply resist.**
  Spoon some resist onto the fabric covering the texture block or material. Pull the resist across the fabric with the plastic spreader to reveal the texture underneath. Reposition the block/material and repeat. Suggested resists: uncooked wheat flour paste, cooked baking powder, gelatin recipe #1. (See C.)

- **Use a dense foam brayer to apply resist.**
  Spoon or squeeze the resist onto a glass palette. Roll a dense foam brayer back and forth across the glass until it is evenly coated with the resist. Roll the brayer over the area of the fabric covering the texture block or material. Reposition the block/material and repeat. Suggested resists: cooked confectioners' sugar, liquid dishwashing soap. (See D.)

Mix a thick dilution of transparent paint. Thicker paint is less likely to breach the resist.

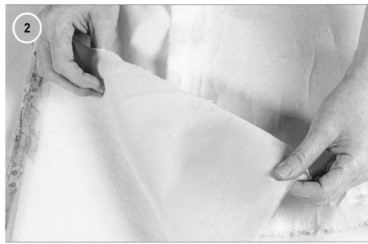

Tape a piece of muslin or cotton onto the portable work surface and tape the fabric with dried resist on top of it.

Apply the paint with a foam brush.

After the paint dries, remove the fabric.

Painting a Resist-Covered Fabric

After the resist completely dries on the fabric, add a wash of transparent paint to reveal the textures and patterns left by the resist. Ideally, the resist prevents the paint from reaching the surface of the fabric. A resist is "breached" when this doesn't occur. We already tried to prevent this from happening by misting the fabric before applying some of the thicker resists. There are four more steps to take to further prevent breaching:

1. A thicker dilution of transparent paint is less likely to seep under the resist. Mix the paint to the consistency of heavy cream. For the paints, I use a ratio of 1 part paint to 1½ parts water.

2. Before applying paint to a resist-covered fabric, sandwich a piece of muslin or cotton between the plastic and the fabric. This helps absorb excess paint and prevents it from pooling on the plastic under the fabric where it can breach the resist.

3. Apply paint with a foam brush. The dried resist acts as a paint barrier. The paint will reach the fabric through cracks or uncovered areas. To further prevent breaching, use a cloth to wipe up excess paint.

4. When the paint is completely dry, remove the fabric from your work surface.

Setting Paint on Resist-Covered Fabric

As mentioned in chapter 1 (see "Setting Paint" on page 22), there are different ways to set paint so it permanently adheres to fabric. Setting fabric paint on resist-covered fabrics requires slight alterations to some of the usual methods. Below are three ways to set the paint.

1. If the brand of fabric paint can be passively set, leave the fabric taped to the padded portable work surface and place in a spot where it will remain undisturbed. After it sits for the determined amount of time needed for the paint to set, follow the directions for removing the resist.

2. To heat-set the paint with an iron, create a fabric "sandwich." Place the painted resist-covered fabric between two cotton or muslin pressing cloths. This protects the iron and ironing surface from direct contact with the resist. Iron the "sandwich" on one side for half the required setting time and then flip it over to iron for the additional time.

3. Put the painted resist-covered fabric in a pillow case and secure with a rubber band or use a cloth (not mesh) drawstring laundry bag. Put the pillow case or laundry bag in the dryer for fifty minutes using the hot setting. Use this technique to heat-set a number of fabrics at the same time.

Removing Resists

After setting the paint, it's time to remove the resist. To do so, follow these steps:

1. Place the set resist-covered fabric in a plastic tub or large bowl that fits in the kitchen sink.

2. Dribble some liquid dishwashing soap on the fabric. (Exception: If the fabric resist used is liquid dishwashing soap, skip this step!)

3. Fill the plastic tub with warm water and let the fabric soak for ten minutes to soften or dissolve the resist.

4. After ten minutes, pour out the "dirty" water and refill the container with more warm water and soap. Let the fabric soak again while swishing it around in the soapy water to further loosen the resist. If there is still resist on the fabric, rub it together under warm running water or scrub gently with a soft toothbrush. Pour out the "dirty" water and repeat until the resist is completely removed.

5. Machine-wash in cold or warm water using the delicate cycle and a small amount of mild detergent. Check the fabric to see whether it needs an additional rinse or machine wash. Dry in a clothes dryer on a light setting or hang dry.

contributing artists

invited a number of artists to try their hand at techniques introduced in this book to see how they might combine them with the surface design techniques they use. I know that they've inspired me to continue on my journey exploring new ways to work with kitchen materials. I hope their creations inspire you as well!

NINE-PATCH FLOWER GARDEN
by Betty C. Ford

Photo by George McClennon

The fabrics for this "flower" garden quilt were created entirely with vegetables and were painted with fabric paints. Betty C. Ford of Rockville, Maryland, has been designing and making art quilts for about twenty years. She has studied with world-famous fiber artists and surface designers for all of those years. http://bettyfordquilts.com

SCARF
by Lisa Chin

Photo by the artist

The scarf was painted with fabric paints. Cardboard tubes with hot glue designs were used to print patterns on the scarf. Lisa Chin is an artist who enjoys exploring with paint, thread, dye, fabric, paper, and anything that will make a mark! Her artwork has been published in national magazines and books and shown in Utah art galleries. http://somethingcleveraboutnothing.blogspot.com, www.etsy.com/shop/somethinglisa

TOTE BAG
by Marilyn Dickey

Photo by the artist

All the patterns on this tote were created with corn, including rolled textures using a corncob with the kernels cut off and sun printing using corn silk. While the painted fabric was drying in the sun, the artist manipulated it to remove some of the fabric paint, leaving bubbles and ridges for more texture. Marilyn Dickey is an editor and writer who enjoys experimenting with fabric design, knitting, crocheting, and other crafts. www.etsy.com/shop/AnneDShop

SMALL BAGS
by Eileen Doughty

Photo by Pam Soorenko

These small bags were designed and created by Eileen Doughty using fabrics printed by Julie B. Booth. Fabric designs were created using brayer rubbings with confectioners' cooked sugar resist. Machine quilted. Eileen Doughty founded Doughty Designs in 1991 and has been creating commissioned work in the textile medium ever since. Her work is in private, public, and corporate collections. www.doughtydesigns.com

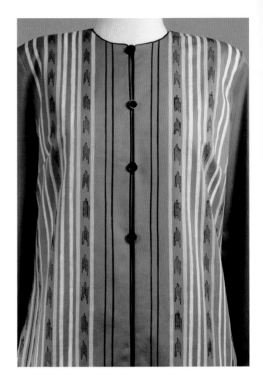

LEILA'S JOURNEY
by Carol R. Eaton

Photo by Pam Soorenko

The original fabric for this table runner was created using an ice dying technique and then layered with flour paste resist. The final design was produced by pulling a comb across the resist-covered fabric and adding circles with a fork. These fabrics were combined with remnants of head scarves worn by Ethiopian women. Carol R. Eaton is a surface design artist who has been creating original, one-of-a-kind fabrics for the past ten years. http://carolreatondesigns.blogspot.com

PILLOW
by Candace Edgerley

Photo by the artist

The fabrics for this pillow were created using hot glue on cardboard bases; adhesive foam cut and mounted on a foam block; and moldable foam fun blocks pressed into a reed mat and hardware washers. Leaf motifs were cut from an easy-cut block. The circle and "x" designs were cut from freezer paper masks. Hand-stitched details using embroidery floss and kantha stitch. Candace Edgerley is an artist whose work has been exhibited both in the United States and internationally. www.candaceedgerley.com

JACKET
by Janet Barnard

Photo by Chris Barnard

Fabrics were hand-stamped with fabric paints using stamps made from layers of spaghetti glued onto foam core in a mock ikat pattern. Lines were stamped from layers of fettuccine glued to foam core and cardboard. The stamps were sealed with a self-leveling acrylic gel for waterproofing. Janet Barnard works from her home studio in Rockville, Maryland. She weaves, paints, and dyes silk and constructs clothing. jbrnrd@comcast.net

PALIMPSEST
by Clara Graves

Photo by Ronald L. Freudenheim

Definition of palimpsest: something having diverse layers apparent beneath the surface. Techniques used to create this wall piece include using oatmeal as a silkscreen resist and stenciling with designs cut from empty cereal boxes and freezer paper. The work was briefly heat-set, then hand-washed, and scrubbed to break up the stenciled surface. Finally black monotypes were printed on silk organza and fused to create the top layer. Clara Graves is a fiber artist whose work is included in private collections around the country. www.claragraves.com

ORANGE CREAM COFFEE CUPS
by Lynn Krawczyk

Photo by Jackie Lams

Printing techniques used for the background of this quilted wall piece include stamping with a radicchio, monoprinting with dried corn, and then stamping with carved squash. The coffee cups were printed with a thermofax screen with marker drawing. The piece was hand-stitched. Lynn Krawczyk is a textile artist, writer, and teacher. http://smudgedtextilesstudio.com

GARMENT
by Ann Liddle

Photo by the artist

This piece involved designs created with torn freezer paper strips ironed to the fabric with fabric paints applied with foam daubers. The colorful strips were cut apart and machine-stitched to black cotton sateen fabric. Ann Liddle has been a studio artist for eighteen years and designs and makes clothing as well as 2D and 3D pieces, using many different techniques and media. www.f-i-n-e.com

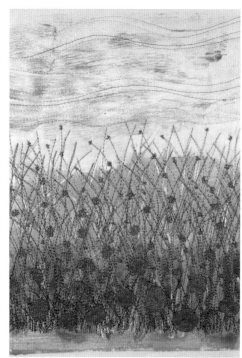

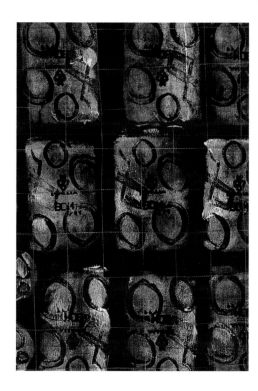

LINENS
by Celina Mancurti

Photo by the artist

This piece includes potato prints on eco-friendly linen. Celina Mancurti is an Argentine textile designer living in the United States. Following her passion for textiles, she decided to work on her own linen collection, which reflects her lifestyle. www.celinamancurti.com, www.etsy.com/shop/CelinaMancurti

POPPIES
by Susan Purney Mark

Photo by the artist

The background fabric for this piece of wall art was monoprinted using a chopstick to create lines of grass in the fabric paint. After the fabric was heat-set, it was fused to a stiff interfacing and then free motion machine-stitched with a variety of decorative threads. Susan Purney Mark has spent the last twenty years learning, experimenting with, and finally teaching a variety of surface design techniques in dyeing, painting, screen printing, and image transfers. She is known for her use of traditional methods with contemporary design and materials. http://susanpm.com

SIMILAR BUT OH SO DIFFERENT
by Lynda Poole Prioleau

Photo by Mark Prioleau

This quilted wall piece was created using recycled foam meat containers. The images were carved into the meat containers using the end of an old paintbrush handle. Fabric paints were used to make the imprints. Lynda Poole Prioleau is a fiber artist who focuses on hand-dyed fabrics, screen printing, and shibori techniques. She creates nontraditional quilts, art wearables, and accessories. www.matlyndesigns.com

CLOUD, PAPER, WATER
by Jennifer Coyne Qudeen

Photo by the artist

This piece was made using a recycled antique Japanese receipt book collaged with cotton fabrics and hand- and machine-stitched. Images were created using a wine cork rolled in paint and then across the surface. Jennifer Coyne Qudeen is a mark maker, storyteller, surface design explorer, rust junkie, and thorough believer in asking, "What if?" www.jennifercoynequdeen.blogspot.com

PURSE
by Lesley Riley

Photo by the artist

An art deco potato masher and a plastic thread spool were printed to create this graphic design. The base fabric is cotton canvas painted with a variety of acrylic and fabric paints. The purse is lined and the leather handles came from bittersweetbasketsandsupply.com. Lesley Riley is an internationally known artist and instructor whose art and articles have appeared in numerous publications and juried shows. She is the author of six books and the originator of TAP Transfer Artist Paper. www.lesleyriley.com

KIMONO-STYLE JACKET
by Priscilla Stultz

Photo by the artist

This Kimono-style jacket is hand-dyed silk printed with recycled cardboard print blocks and kitchen staples. Print blocks included string wrapped around cardboard, cut cardboard shapes glued to cardboard bases, and rice glued to a cardboard base. The jacket is lined with hand-dyed fabrics. Priscilla Stultz is an award-winning fiber and wearable artist living in Virginia. She has watched her designs walk the runway, get exhibited in shows and museums, and travel the country. www.priscillastultz.com

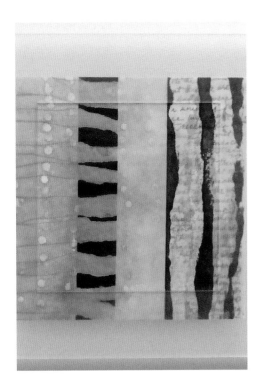

GATHERING DREAMS SERIES—OCEAN CHANNELS
by Pam Sullivan

Photo by the artist

Transparent fabric paints were applied over torn freezer paper masks and screen printing on nonwoven polyester fabric in this machine-stitched piece. This triptych is about the mysteries of the oceans and the stories and information that are continually surfacing from the deep. Pam Sullivan has exhibited in group and solo shows across the United States. Her mixed media and fiber work is about time and place, nature, and our interconnected role. www.pamsullivan.com

PILLOW
by Helga Elli Thomas

Photo by the artist

Large and small paint dots were applied to the fabric using a whittled chopstick (found object printing). The leaf designs were monoprinted using sage leaves as stencils. Helga Elli Thomas is the owner of Adobe Trader Studio, a modern textile design studio creating unique handcrafted works of art via fabric. Her work is inspired by the natural colors, intricate patterns, and landscapes of the earth. All of her decorative textile products are one-of-a-kind pieces that she designs, paints, and stencils by hand. Fabrics and paints are people, animal, and environmentally friendly. www.etsy.com/shop/AdobeTrader

TOURIST GO HOME
by Jessica Todd

Photo by the artist

This piece was created in multiple steps using salt resist, freezer paper masks, and print blocks. Tourist Go Home was inspired by graffiti encountered during a trip to Seville, Spain. The artist wanted to contrast the beautiful antique Spanish tile design and romanticized image of Spain with the harsh and palpable graffiti message to tourists. Jessica Todd is a contemporary craft artist whose MFA work was in jewelry, metals, and enameling at Kent State University. She also frequently incorporates textiles and other media into her work. http://jesstoddstudio.com, www.etsy.com/shop/jesstodd

resources

Below are the suppliers I use for fabric, paints, and tools.

ONLINE SOURCES

Dharma Trading Co.
www.dharmatrading.com
800-542-5227

Dick Blick Art Materials
www.dickblick.com
800-828-4548

Mister Art
www.misterart.com
800-721-3015

RECOMMENDED BOOKS

Surface Design Techniques: General

Off-the-Shelf Fabric Painting: 30 Simple Recipes for Gourmet Results
Sue Beevers
C&T Publishing, 2004.

Fabric Painting for Embroidery
Valerie Campbell-Harding
Batsford, 1990.

Transforming Fabric: 30 Creative Ways to Paint, Dye and Pattern Cloth
Carolyn A. Dahl
Krause Publications, 2004.

Art Cloth: A Guide to Surface Design for Fabric
Jane Dunnewold
Interweave Press, 2010.

Complex Cloth: A Comprehensive Guide to Surface Design
Jane Dunnewold
Fiber Studio Press, 1996.

Create Your Own Hand-Printed Cloth: Stamp, Screen & Stencil with Everyday Objects
Rayna Gillman
C&T Publishing, 2008.

The Textile Design Book: Understanding and Creating Patterns Using Texture, Shape and Color
Karin Jerstorp and Eva Kohlmark
Lark Books, 1988.

Mickey Lawler's Sky Dyes: A Visual Guide to Fabric Painting
Mickey Lawler
C&T Publishing, 1999.

Colors Changing Hue
Yvonne Porcella
C&T Publishing, 1994.

Surface Design for Fabric
Richard M. Proctor and Jennifer F. Lew
University of Washington Press, 1995.

Mastering the Art of Fabric Printing and Design: Techniques, Tutorials, and Inspiration
Laurie Wisbrun
Chronicle Books, 2011.

Specific Technique Books

STAMPING AND PRINTING

Great Impressions: The Art & Technique of Rubber Stamping
Patricia Garner Berlin
Flower Valley Press, 1997.

Nature Printing with Herbs, Fruits & Flowers
Laura Donnelly Bethmann
Storey Communications, Inc., 1996.

Print & Stamp Lab
Traci Bunkers
Quarry Books, 2010.

Print, Pattern & Colour
Ruth Issett
Batsford, 2007.

RESIST TECHNIQUES

Visual Texture on Fabric: Creating Stunning Art Cloth with Water-Based Resists
Lisa Kerpoe
C&T Publishing, 2012.

INSPIRATIONS—DESIGN AND COMPOSITION

Finding Your Own Visual Language: A Practical Guide to Design & Composition
Jane Dunnewold, Claire Benn & Leslie Morgan
Committed to Cloth, 2007.

NOTAN: The Dark-Light Principle of Design
Dorr Bothwell and Marlys Mayfield
Dover Publications, Inc., 1991.

PATTERNS AND DESIGNS FOR PRINT BLOCKS/STENCILS

Designer's Guide to Japanese Patterns: Book 2
Jeanne Allen
Chronicle Books, 1988.

Designer's Guide to Japanese Patterns: Book 3
Jeanne Allen
Chronicle Books, 1989.

Design Motifs of Ancient Mexico
Jorge Enciso
Dover Publications, Inc., 1953.

4000 Animal, Bird & Fish Motifs: A Sourcebook
Graham Leslie McCallum
Batsford, 2005.

4000 Flower & Plant Motifs: A Sourcebook
Graham Leslie McCallum
Batsford, 2004.

Pattern Motifs: A Sourcebook
Graham Leslie McCallum
Batsford, 2006.

Pattern Sourcebook: Nature
Shigeki Nakamura
Rockport Publishers, 2009.

Pattern Sourcebook: Nature 2
Shigeki Nakamura
Rockport Publishers, 2009.

African Designs from Traditional Sources
Geoffrey Williams
Dover Publications, Inc., 1971.

North American Indian Designs for Artists and Craftspeople
Eva Wilson
Dover Publications, Inc., 1984.

The Art of Decorative Paper Stencils
Kanako Yaguchi
Quarry Books, 2007.

acknowledgments

Many people helped make this book possible.

Thank you to Mary Ann Hall for recognizing the potential in this book idea and encouraging me to "tweak" it a bit.

A very special thanks to my two editors: Tiffany Hill for her contagious enthusiasm and spot-on editing. And to Cara Connors for her careful attention to detail and endless patience in helping me see this project through to completion.

Thank you, Pam Soorenko, for the gorgeous photography. I enjoyed our photo shoots and your imaginative viewpoint from behind the camera lens.

Thank you, Regina Grenier and John Foster, for the enticing book cover and page design that literally draws readers in.

To all the artists who contributed work to the gallery chapter, my heartfelt thanks. When the call went out for artwork, you all enthusiastically offered to produce pieces incorporating techniques presented in this book. Your artwork is truly spectacular and has opened my eyes even wider to the inherent potential to be found in these techniques.

A special thanks goes out to my mentor and art coach, Lesley Riley. You helped me realize that with hard work, determination, and some courage, my dream of becoming an author could become a reality.

A loving thanks to my husband, Mark, for your pep talks, hugs, and meatloaf.

And to all my family and friends, thank you for your encouraging words and demands for signed book copies!

about the author

Julie B. Booth started stitching and printing at a young age. She took up embroidery needle and thread at the age of ten and spent many Saturday nights in high school happily carving linoleum blocks.

In 1994, Julie launched her business, Thread Born Dolls, specializing in creating one-of-a-kind cloth dolls and doll patterns. She soon rediscovered printing, this time on fabric. Julie's hand-printed fabrics soon became a recognizable hallmark of all her artistic creations. In 2010, she was asked to design a line of hand-printed fabrics for the home furnishings arm of Caos on F Gallery in Washington, DC.

Julie is a member of F.I.N.E. (Fiber in Nearly Everything), an exhibiting group of seven mixed media fiber artists as well as a longtime member of both the Potomac Fiber Arts Guild and Potomac Fiber Arts Gallery. Most recently, she joined nine other surface design enthusiasts (the "Hive") in The Printed Fabric Bee, where each month members create and share unique printed fabrics.

An enthusiastic fiber arts educator, Julie specializes in teaching classes in surface design, doll making, and embellishment techniques. She loves to encourage her students to be fearless, open-minded, and willing to explore.

In 2010, Julie received a grant to study using common household materials as fabric resists. Most of her research took place in the kitchen, where she concocted fabric resists from ingredients that ranged from gelatin to baking powder. Realizing that the kitchen holds many more surface design surprises, Julie continues to play in the kitchen. In 2012, she started her blog, *Julie B Booth Surface Design*, and a monthly online newsletter, *Julie B Booth Surface Design News*, dedicated to exploring kitchen-inspired surface design. In addition to raiding the kitchen for art supplies, Julie's recent interests include using printed fabrics to tell a story and stitching cloth as a form of healing. Visit Julie's blog, www.threadbornblog.com or view her artwork at www.threadborn.com.

index

A

adhesives, 25

aluminum cans/pans, 92–93

aluminum foil, 72–75

B

backgrounds
  painting, 16–17, 33
  vegetable textures, 50–51

baker's clay, 38–39

baking powder resist, 99

Bernard, Janet, 116

block designs, 34–41

brayer rubbing, 30, 42–43, 59, 74

C

cabbage prints, 52–53

cardboard, 78–82, 108

cardboard tubes, 88–89, 95

carrots, 53

cellophane window stencils, 87

Chin, Lisa, 115

cleaning tools, 22

clothing catalogs, 84, 87

collage design, 30–33

confectioners' sugar resist, 102

corncob printing, 49

craft knife-cut designs, 62

cutting tools, 25

D

Dickey, Marilyn, 115

dimensional print blocks, 43

direct printing, 30, 94

dishwashing soap resist, 103–104

Doughty, Eileen, 115

drying fabrics, 22

E

Eaton, Carol R., 116

Edgerley, Candace, 116

embossed designs
  accentuating, 92
  aluminum cans/pans, 92
  aluminum foil, 72–75
  embossed baker's clay blocks, 38–39

equipment, 25
  See also tools

erasers, 44–46

F

fabric
  backgrounds, 16–17, 33, 50–51
  choices and sizes, 13, 15

drying, 22
   resist-covered, painting, 112–113
fabric paint, 13, 15, 22
fabric resists. *See* resists
flour paste resist, 98
foam brayer, 18, 108, 111
foam brush, 19
foam dauber, 20–21, 67
foam material, 90–91
fold-and-scissor-cut designs, 62
folk art fabric design, 74–75
Ford, Betty C., 114
found object printing, 29–47
freezer paper, 61–67
   applying paint to, 66–67
   masks, 62–63, 110
   stencils, 64–65
fruit designs, 49, 57

G
gelatin resist, 99–101
glass monoprint, 108
Graves, Clara, 117

H
hot glue blocks, 81

I
inventory, 30

J
junk mail, 84–87

K
kitchen ingredients, 97–113
kitchen textures, 29–47, 108
Krawczyk, Lynn, 117

L
layered textures, 30–33
leaves, 58–59, 108
Liddle, Ann, 117
liquid dishwashing soap resist, 103–104

M
Mancurti, Celina, 118
marbled fabric, 52–53
Mark, Susan Purney, 118
marking tools, 25
masks
   freezer paper, 62–63, 110
   vs. stencils, 63
materials, 12–15, 30
   See also tools

measuring tools, 25
monoprint on glass, 108

O
opaque fabric paints, 17

P
padded portable work surface, 13–14
paint/painting
   backgrounds, 16–17, 33
   fabric, 13, 15–17
   foam brayer, 18, 108, 111
   foam brush, 19
   foam dauber, 20–21, 67
   freezer paper, 66–67
   mixing custom colors, 15, 17, 51
   opaque, 17
   pastel effects, 67
   resist-covered fabric, 112–113
   setting, 22, 113
   techniques, 15, 18–21
   transparent, 15–17
   using, 51
   watercolor effects, 66
paper, 25
pastel effects, 67
pencil erasers, 44, 46

plastic spreader, 108, 111

plastic wrap, 68–69

postcards, 85

Prepared for Dyeing (PFD) cotton, 13

print blocks

    block designs, 34–41

    cardboard, 78–79

    dimensional, 43

    foam, 91

    from vegetables, 54–57

printed sampler, 55

printing, 30

    brayer rubbing, 30, 42–43, 59, 74

    with cardboard tubes, 95

    collage design, 33

    direct, 30, 94

    with foam brayer, 18, 108

    with leaves, 108

    with plastic spreader, 108

    with recycled materials, 94–95

    with resists, 108–111

    stenciling, 30

    texture blocks, 40–41

    with vegetable shapes, 56–57

printing plate

    aluminum foil, 72–75

    for brayer rubbings, 74

wax paper, 70–71

Prioleau, Lynda Poole, 118

Q

Qudeen, Jennifer Coyne, 119

R

recycled materials, 77–95

    aluminum cans/pans, 92–93

    cardboard, 78–82

    cardboard tubes, 88–89, 95

    foam, 90–91

    junk mail, 84–87

    printing with, 94–95

resists, 97–113

    about, 97

    application techniques, 105–107

    cooked baking powder, 99

    cooked confectioners' sugar, 102

    on flat kitchen textures, 108

    freezer paper masks, 110

    gelatin, 99–101

    liquid dishwashing soap, 103–104

    painting resist-covered fabric, 112–113

    printing with, 108–111

    recipes, 98–103

    removing, 113

rubbings, 111
    stencils, 108–109
    uncooked wheat flour paste, 98
Riley, Lesley, 119
rubber band block, 36
rubbings, 30, 42–43, 59, 74, 111

S

shaped erasers, 45
small-scale items, 46–47
stencils, 30, 31
    cardboard, 82–83, 108
    cellophane window, 87
    freezer paper, 64–65
    vs. masks, 63
    resists, 108–109
string block, 37
Stultz, Priscilla, 119
Sullivan, Pam, 120
supplies, 12–15, 24–27

T

tear designs, 62
textures
    backgrounds, 50–51
    brayer rubbings, 42–43
    embossed baker's clay blocks, 38–39

kitchen, 29–47, 108
    layered, 30–33
    material suggestions, 30
    texture blocks, 34–43
    vegetables, 50–51
Thomas, Helga Elli, 120
Todd, Jessica, 120
toolkit, 12–15
tools, 22, 24–27
transparent fabric paint, 15, 16–17
twine block, 37
twist-tie block, 36

U

uncooked wheat flour paste resist, 98
upholstery foam, 43

V

vegetable designs, 49–59
    background textures, 50–51
    carrots, 53
    leaves, 58–59
    marbled fabric, 52–53
    print blocks, 54–57

W

watercolor effects, 66

wax paper, 70–71
workspace
    padded portable, 13–14
    setting up, 11, 13
wraps and papers, 61–75
    aluminum foil, 72–75
    freezer paper, 61–67
    plastic wrap, 68–69
    wax paper, 70–71

Don't miss these other books on fabric art!

Fabric Art Workshop

Susan Stein

ISBN: 978-1-58923-663-9

Tangle Stitches for Quilters and Fabric Artists

Jane Monk

ISBN: 978-1-58923-797-1

Print and Stamp Lab

Traci Bunkers

ISBN: 978-1-59253-598-9

Print and Stamp Lab: A Creative Art Kit

Traci Bunkers

ISBN: 978-1-59253-930-7

Our books are available as E-Books, too!

Many of our bestselling titles are now available as E-Books. Visit www.Qbookshop.com to find links to e-vendors!